Advance praise for *7 Secrets of Persuasion*

"*7 Secrets of Persuasion* is accessible, smart, and important. Jim Crimmins has distilled his years of experience as a professional persuader and advertiser into a book on how to develop compelling and persuasive messages…it is well worth our attention."

—Ellen Wartella, chair, Department of Communication Studies, Northwestern University and Professor of Psychology

"This is great stuff. Your clear and concise translation of these principles is something every public health communicator should be exposed to."

—Matthew Kreuter, Kahn Family Professor of Public Health, Associate Dean for Public Health, senior scientist, Health Communication Research Laboratory, Washington University in St. Louis

7 SECRETS OF PERSUASION

Leading-Edge Neuromarketing Techniques
to Influence Anyone

By James C. Crimmins, PhD

CAREER
PRESS

Wayne, NJ

7 SECRETS OF PERSUASION
EDITED BY ROGER SHEETY
TYPESET BY DIANA GHAZZAWI

Cover design by Howard Grossman/12E Design
Printed in the U.S.A.

To order this title, please call toll-free 1-800-CAREER-1 (NJ and Canada: 201-848-0310) to order using VISA or MasterCard, or for further information on books from Career Press.

CAREER
PRESS

The Career Press, Inc.
12 Parish Drive
Wayne, NJ 07470
www.careerpress.com

Library of Congress Cataloging-in-Publication Data

CIP Data Available Upon Request.

For Rita

CONTENTS

FOREWORD

Anyone who wishes to persuade a child, a boss, a partner, a spouse, or a customer in a showroom should read this book. The principles of persuasion Jim Crimmins reveals on the pages that follow apply in any situation where individuals need to be persuaded to do something they are not doing or, conversely, to be persuaded not to do something they are already doing.

As a longtime practitioner of advertising, I wish Jim had written this book years ago when I was still working day to day in the business of creating campaigns for clients and trying to get them to understand what we intuitively knew: Consumers may rationalize a brand choice, but the choice is really driven by their emotions. People don't choose a brand based on facts and rational arguments any more than they choose a life partner or a political candidate that way. Instead, they base their purchase decisions pretty much on their feelings about a brand, feelings created in large part by the brand's advertising. That's why, as Jim so convincingly points out in this book, asking people why they do things is not only a mistake, it will take you down the wrong path. It turns out that people actually don't know why they do certain things; so, in trying to tell you, they'll misguide you. Instead of asking them, Jim urges us to "unearth" people's true motivations, and he shares some proven ways to do that.

It's a shame that we in advertising, when I was still involved in the work every day and even now, have never been able to fully explain how our product works, how advertising can attach real values and set expectations that actually transform the experience of using a brand. Nor have we always been able to prove that the most persuasive advertising may present no rational argument at all. It's sad to think about so many potentially great campaigns rejected by clients who, in the absence of the kind of scientific evidence contained in this book, were conned by copy testers with bogus systems into believing that the measure of success for advertising was a respondent's ability to recall copy points or play back a brand's so-called "unique selling proposition." We have always felt passionately that real persuasion is more about a "unique selling personality"—how a brand looks and feels and acts, what a brand does rather than what it says, indeed what a brand's "body language" conveys. But we have always been at a loss to prove such a point of view and so some of the very best ideas have gone down in flames.

That's because until now, we weren't armed with the groundbreaking discoveries made by the new science of the mind detailed in this book. Within these pages, Jim details dozens of recent scientific studies that prove in various ways how and why a reasoned argument can be a waste of time and why, to be successful as persuaders, we must get to know the "lizard," which is Jim's way of describing the brain's automatic, nonconscious mental system that acts without deliberate thinking. Apparently, we share this ancient system with lizards and all other vertebrates. And according to evidence Jim presents, this system makes the key decisions when the brain selects one brand, or one proposition, or one person over another.

Jim Crimmins speaks from his years of experience as a top strategist for advertising agencies Needham, Harper & Steers and DDB Worldwide. He is an expert on the subject of human behavior and he fills the pages of this book with both positive and negative examples, gleaned from his own experience and the related experience of others. Throughout the book, Jim surprises us with new insights in the same enlightening way I came to depend upon during the years we worked together. For example, in one chapter, he turns on its head the idea that attitude change must precede behavior change. With examples, readers are shown why would-be persuaders should aim at the act they wish to change, not the attitude. The attitude change, according to Jim, will follow.

At a time when the advertising industry often seems more obsessed with clicks than with true connections, the revelations found in this book are both timely and empowering. In fact, now that Jim Crimmins has provided us with scientific evidence that persuasion is more about feelings than facts, I may go back and try to sell some of those potentially great campaigns that eschewed rational arguments in favor of emotional appeal. They're still sitting, rejected, on the shelf. But having read Jim Crimmins's book, I feel certain the lizard would like them.

—Keith Reinhard

1

GETTING TO KNOW
THE LIZARD

Whether persuading your boss, your kids, or your spouse, or persuading millions to eat healthier foods, to vote for your candidate, or to choose a Galaxy phone, persuasion often fails. A better understanding of the mind improves the chance of success.

Recent discoveries in psychology, behavioral economics, and neuroscience dramatically expand what we know about how we choose and should change how we attempt to persuade. We've learned that consciousness is not central to most of our decisions. It feels central, but scientific evidence shows that consciousness usually takes a back seat. This turns the conventional wisdom of persuasion on its head and may explain why persuasion attempts, whether of one person or of many, often don't work.

As a professional persuader for 27 years—mainly as Chief Strategic Officer of DDB Chicago and a Worldwide Brand Planning Director—I was in charge of analyzing what should work, what did work, and what didn't work for such clients as Budweiser, Dell, Discover Card, and Westin. I found myself puzzled by both failures and successes, and spent a great deal of time trying to figure out what made an advertisement go one way or another. The conventional wisdom of advertising didn't seem to apply. As I studied the latest research into our brains and our decision-making, I began to see why. I became intrigued with scientists who, for the first time, were shedding light on the dark matter of the mind. I could see why the traditional approach to advertising failed and how we had to update our ideas on persuasion.

This book takes the latest scientific insights about the mind and applies them to the art of persuasion. Until now, persuasion has been hit or miss because would-be persuaders didn't understand how we choose. But thanks to the groundbreaking research of such scientists as Daniel Kahneman, Amos Tversky, and others beginning 40 years ago, in what has been a revolution in mind science, today we better understand how we make decisions. I translate this revolution into practical techniques for successful persuasion. These techniques will help anyone become more persuasive, whether the goal is to influence one person—a relative, friend, or colleague—or the many who might purchase an Apple Watch or a Chevy.

We have two different ways of thinking: (1) the automatic system—our nonconscious mental processes, and (2) the reflective system—our conscious mental processes. We now know the automatic system affects all our choices and is the sole influence in many. The roots of our automatic, nonconscious mental system lie in ancient brain structures we share with lizards and, indeed, all vertebrates. Although the degree of development of the nonconscious mind varies considerably across species, its basic function remains the same: to pursue pleasure and avoid pain. The automatic mental system is what Richard Thaler and Cass Sunstein referred to as the lizard inside.[1]

Thaler, Sunstein, and I don't mean to disparage the automatic, nonconscious mental system by calling it the lizard inside. Thanks to our automatic system we can walk, talk, understand the input of our senses, develop likes and dislikes, choose friends, and fall in love. The lizard is smart and intuitive. It's who we are when we aren't thinking about it. The lizard acts without conscious deliberation, instantly, effortlessly, and can't be turned off.

The lizard looks at life differently than our conscious mental system.

- For the lizard, what comes most easily to mind seems most true. The lizard can't tell the difference between familiarity and accuracy.

- For the lizard, people are what they do no matter why they do it. The lizard focuses on action and ignores motivation.

- Because of the lizard, persuasion should aim at the act rather than the attitude, as behavior is easier to change.

- Because of the lizard, we should never ask people why they do what they do. People don't know why, but they think they do. You can find out what you need to know, but you won't find out by asking.

- The lizard is partial to immediate, certain, and emotional rewards, but good-for-you choices like dieting, saving money, or stopping smoking offer the opposite. Understanding the lizard allows you to transform rewards, changing the delayed into the immediate, the uncertain into the certain, and the rational into the emotional.

The seven secrets of persuasion revealed in this book are not a collection of separate techniques that you need to choose among. You can use any one, two, or all of them whenever you attempt to persuade, whether you seek to persuade one or many, and whether the goal is important or trivial.

The secrets of persuasion succeed by dealing with the lizard.

The Lizard

You may have a spouse. You very likely have a religion. You certainly have a number of friends. How did you choose them?

Did you evaluate each person relative to others on their spouse-potential? Did you analyze all religions and choose the one you found most compelling? Do you remember considering the wide range of people you know and selecting certain individuals to be your friends?

Of course not; no one does. Even though these choices may be the most important decisions of your life, you didn't go through any conscious process to make them. You made the choices. You just don't know exactly how.

We don't make choices the way we think we do. We think we consciously consider the options and we believe we know why we pick one option over the others. It doesn't work that way. No matter how it feels, consciousness is not crucial to most of our decisions. Our conscious mind is often on the periphery of our choices.

In the words of Jonathan Miller in the *New York Review of Books*, "Human beings owe a surprisingly large proportion of their cognitive and behavioral capacities to the existence of an 'automatic self' of which they have no conscious knowledge and over which they have little voluntary control."[2]

For most choices, our nonconscious, automatic mental system, the lizard inside, is in charge. To persuade the lizard, we must understand it and speak its language.

David Eagleman is a neuroscientist at Baylor College of Medicine, where he directs both the Laboratory for Perception and Action and the Initiative on Neuroscience and Law. In his book, *Incognito: The Secret Lives of the Brain*, Eagleman tells us that the realization that consciousness is not central to behavior is as radical as the realization that the earth is not the center of the solar system.[3] Derision, anger, and prosecution met Galileo's announcement. The Vatican censored his works for 200 years.

To people in the 17th century, it was obvious that the earth was the center of the solar system. They could feel it in their bones when the sun passed overhead each day. It seems just as clear to us that consciousness is central to our behavior. But, in both cases, scientific evidence to the contrary is undeniable.

Sigmund Freud first brought attention to the unconscious. He understood the importance of our nonconscious processes, but he misunderstood their nature. Freud believed that the unconscious contained primitive urges for sex and aggression that are so powerful we need to keep them out of awareness. What we understand today about mental processes outside of conscious awareness is far from the roiling set of embarrassing desires that come to mind when most people think of Freud's unconscious.

Contemporary psychologists do not want their work on nonconscious processes to share the connotations of the Freudian unconscious. They have generally avoided the term "unconscious" and referred to nonconscious processes as "implicit," "pre-attentive," or "subconscious." Unfortunately, these labels suggest our nonconscious system is somehow less important than our conscious system.

Daniel Kahneman solved that problem by calling nonconscious processes, or "thinking fast," System 1, and calling conscious processes, or "thinking slow," System 2.[4] But System 1 and System 2 make it too hard to keep track of which is conscious and which is nonconscious.

Thaler and Sunstein used labels that are both descriptive and memorable. Richard Thaler, an economist at the University of Chicago, working with Cass Sunstein, a prolific legal scholar at Harvard Law School, wrote their best-selling *Nudge* to show how the science of choice could be used to nudge people toward decisions that will make their lives better.[5] Thaler and Sunstein describe nonconscious processes as the "automatic system" and conscious processes as the "reflective system."

I'll borrow from Thaler and Sunstein and refer to our nonconscious mental processes as the automatic system (that is, the lizard inside) and refer to our conscious mental processes as the reflective system. Automatic and reflective are clear and avoid suggesting that nonconscious processes are subordinate.

Both the automatic and reflective mental systems are active whenever we are awake. The lizard inside, the automatic, nonconscious mental system, usually takes the lead generating impressions, feelings, inclinations, and impulses whereas our reflective, conscious mental system goes along with the automatic system's suggestions unless provoked.

The mental system outside of our awareness is much more influential than we realize, having a powerful influence on all our choices and judgments. Our automatic, nonconscious mental system, the lizard inside, not only influences the options we choose, but also plays a key role, often the sole role, in originating any action we take.

Our reflective, conscious system is important in some actions, especially those for which we were not well prepared by evolution like dieting, calculus, and science, or not well prepared by frequent repetition or habit like finding our way in an unfamiliar city, or following the protocol of meeting royalty.

The automatic system, the lizard inside, directs all those internal procedures that keep us alive—blood pumping, breathing, digestion. But that is just the beginning. Our automatic, nonconscious mental system enables us to understand what we see or hear turning the massive amounts of data coming in through our senses into understandable patterns. Our automatic system allows us to speak and stay upright and catch a fly ball. Because all these wondrous operations take place outside of conscious awareness, we find it hard to give credit. Eagleman compares our conscious mind to "…a tiny stowaway on a transatlantic steamship, taking credit for the journey without acknowledging the massive engineering underfoot."[6]

In order to succeed at persuasion we have to deal with the lizard inside, the automatic mental system. We have to learn how the lizard works and how it can be influenced.

Psychologists, neuroscientists, and behavior economists have spelled out the differences between the reflective, conscious mental system and the automatic, nonconscious mental system. The following chart summarizes the differences.[7]

Table 1.1: Reflective Versus Automatic Mental Systems

Reflective, Conscious System	Automatic, Nonconscious System (The Lizard Inside)
Single module	Multiple modules
Slow and deliberate	Fast
Small capacity	Enormous capacity
Effortful	Effortless
Intentional but lazy	Unintentional and cannot be turned off
Taking the long view	Concerned with the here and now
Capable of learning new tasks	Capable of performing innate tasks or tasks in which we have become expert through prolonged practice

The reflective, conscious mental system has one module. Our conscious mental system is either on or off. We are either conscious or we are not.

The automatic, nonconscious mental system consists of multiple modules. Our automatic mental system guides many largely independent activities—digestion, circulation, breathing, depth perception, balance, language, and so on. Patients with brain damage can completely lose certain capabilities, like depth perception, whereas other capabilities, like language, function normally.

The reflective system is slow and deliberate, but the automatic system is fast. A study by psychologists at Northwestern University illustrated the speed of the automatic, nonconscious system relative to the reflective, conscious system.[8]

Participants were shown on a computer screen human faces expressing surprise. Unbeknownst to the participants, before they saw the surprised faces, they were shown, for 30 milliseconds, faces either with fearful expressions or happy expressions. At 30 milliseconds, or 3/100 of a second, the fearful or happy expressions were too brief for participants to be consciously aware of them.

Participants then rated the surprised faces from "extremely positive" to "extremely negative."

Participants who unconsciously saw the initial fearful micro-expressions rated the surprised faces more negatively than participants who unconsciously saw the initial happy micro-expressions.

The automatic, nonconscious system saw the initial faces shown for 3/100 of a second, interpreted the meaning, and provided consciousness with an inclination that influenced conscious perception even though consciousness had no idea the initial pictures were shown.

When we meet new people, their faces often reveal, for an instant, their pleasure or lack of pleasure in meeting us. After that instant, which is too fast for our conscious mind to pick up, their polite smiles are in place. But our automatic system catches the instantaneous expressions and leaves us with a vaguely positive or negative feeling about the new people.

These psychologists suggest that we continually, automatically, and unconsciously scan the environment for threats. In searching for threats, speed is essential.

Imagine you are a salesperson in a Ford showroom and a man walks in the door thinking about buying a car. If you don't genuinely like that potential buyer even before he walks in, you are already in a hole. The buyer instantly, effortlessly, and without even knowing it, senses what you think of him. What he senses will affect your entire interaction. If you want to sell more cars, work on genuinely liking people even before you meet them. Will Rogers said, "I never yet met a man that I dident like."[9] Will would have been a heck of a salesman.

I recently bought a car and didn't analyze the experience at the time. But when my wife asked me about it, I realized that I had gotten the immediate impression that the salesman in the first dealership thought very highly of himself and a lot less highly of me. He may have been right, but he seemed to form that judgment even before he met me. It soured the interaction and I bought the car somewhere else.

The reflective, conscious mental system has limited capacity, whereas the automatic, nonconscious mental system has enormous capacity. Scientists have estimated the capacity of our mental systems. By examining our ability to distinguish sounds, smells, tastes, and stimuli to the skin, as well as the number of linguistic bits we can process when we read or listen, scientists estimate that our reflective, conscious mental system can process about 40 pieces of information a second.

They have also gotten a good idea of the bandwidth of our automatic, nonconscious mental system by counting how many nerve connections send signals to the brain and how many signals each connection sends a second. The eyes alone send 10 million pieces of information to the brain every second. The rest of our senses together—touch, sound, smell, taste—send more than one million more pieces of information every second. In other words, our nonconscious mental system processes the 11,000,000 pieces of information per second that are submitted by our senses.

The difference in the estimated capacity of the two mental systems is so large that some might doubt the accuracy of the estimates. But even if those estimates are way off, the capacity of the automatic, nonconscious system still dwarfs the capacity of the reflective, conscious system. If the actual capacity of the automatic, nonconscious mental system is one-third the current scientific estimate and the actual capacity of the reflective, conscious mental system is three times greater than the current scientific estimate, the capacity of the automatic system is still 25,000 times larger than the capacity of the reflective system.

Our automatic, nonconscious mental system uses that massive capacity to do triage. The lizard observes the deluge of incoming information—deciding what to ignore, what to leave up to automatic processes, and what to pass into consciousness (see Norretranders[10]). Our automatic, nonconscious mental system processes the flood of incoming information, most of which does not even enter our consciousness. In handling this information, our automatic system can do much more than we imagine.

Pawel Lewicki established the Nonconscious Information Processing Laboratory at the University of Tulsa. Working with his colleagues, Lewicki illustrated the remarkable ability of the automatic, nonconscious mental system with a simple experiment.[11] Participants looked at a computer screen divided into four quadrants. Periodically, an "X" would appear in one of the quadrants and the participant pressed one of four keys to indicate the quadrant in which the "X" appeared. Though the participants did not know it, the sequence of quadrants in which the "X" appeared followed a complex pattern. For example, the "X" would never return to a particular quadrant until it had first appeared in at least two of the other quadrants. Because of its complexity, no participant consciously realized there was a pattern.

The experimenters timed how long it took from appearance of the "X" until the key was pressed indicating in which quadrant it appeared. The time from appearance of the "X" until the key was pressed is a measure of the ease or difficulty of the task. With repetition, participants became faster and faster indicating that they had nonconsciously learned the underlying complex pattern. When the pattern changed, participants' speed slowed because they could no longer nonconsciously anticipate where the "X" would appear. Participants in the experiment clearly learned the underlying pattern, but they consciously had no idea that there was an underlying pattern, no idea that they learned it, and no idea why their speed slowed when the pattern changed.

Our automatic, nonconscious mental system has access to far more information than our reflective system and our automatic system is quite skilled at interpreting that information.

Our automatic system, in the words of neuroscientists, is capable of "Deciding Advantageously Before Knowing the Advantageous Strategy."[12] In an experiment that illustrated this point, scientists at the University of Iowa asked participants to turn over cards from one of four decks placed before them in a simulated gambling task. Most of the time, turning over a card led to a reward, but occasionally and unpredictably, a card led to a loss. Participants had no way of knowing that two of the decks were more risky than the others. Participants began to avoid the risky decks shortly after the experiment began, even before they consciously knew which decks were risky. In fact, their perspiration revealed that these participants began to feel emotionally uncomfortable whenever they thought about choosing a card from a risky deck even before they consciously knew it was a risky choice. The automatic, nonconscious mental system sensed risk before the reflective system was conscious of it. The automatic system communicated that risk and influenced choice through emotion.

Our automatic, nonconscious mental system has the capability to take advantage of patterns that are so complex or so subtle that they never even reach the awareness of our reflective, conscious system.

Reflective, conscious thinking is effortful. Automatic, nonconscious thinking is effortless. To illustrate this point, imagine you wish to calculate the product of 57 times 75. This requires conscious effort and attention. By contrast, carrying on a conversation in our native language is effortless. We don't have to try to understand what someone is saying to us. In fact, we can't turn the automatic system off. We understand what someone is saying even if we don't want to.

When we realize how much work it is to carry on a conversation in a language we are starting to learn, we see that conversation is a marvelous mental feat.

With long and repeated effort, we can develop the facility to make conversation in another language effortless. The reflective, conscious system can pass a task over to our automatic system when much repetition makes the task easy. Bicycle riding and piano playing (for the accomplished pianist) are additional examples of tasks that can be so well learned that they become effortless and pass over to the automatic, nonconscious mental system.

Our reflective, conscious system operates only when we intend it to operate. It is intentional and only occasionally engaged. Our automatic, nonconscious system operates whether we want it to or not. It is unintentional and inexorable.

Our reflective, conscious mental system generally relaxes in the background of our thinking and only takes charge when it focuses on a task that the automatic system can't handle, such as filling out a tax return. On the other hand, our automatic, nonconscious mental system is actively engaged whenever we are awake. We can't really shut it off. If we look out the window, we cannot avoid arranging the many millions of light impressions received into a coherent 3D image.

Most of the time, our lazy conscious mental system will accept the suggestions of the lizard and go on.

Our deliberate system takes the long view and can plan for the future. Our automatic system is only concerned about the here and now.

Our reflective, conscious mental system can anticipate what's ahead, imagine the conditions, and decide to save. Our automatic, nonconscious mental system cannot encourage us to save for retirement because it doesn't think about what the future will hold. The lizard inside deals with immediate gratification.

Our deliberate, conscious mental system is capable of learning new tasks. Our automatic, nonconscious mental system performs tasks that are innate, or habitual, or in which we have become expert through sustained repetition.

We are already familiar with our reflective system because it is the us we know. The reflective system gives rise to agriculture, science, technology, and most anything we might learn in school. But, on a daily basis, our automatic system is in charge of most of our actions. We are not familiar with the automatic, nonconscious mental system because, by definition, its workings take place outside of consciousness.

This book emphasizes the automatic mental system because its role in everyday actions makes it the most promising target for persuasion attempts.

Persuasion's Two Challenges

The first challenge is to get someone to do something that they might otherwise not do. For example, you might want a potential voter who is partial to your candidate to actually vote instead of staying home, or you might want someone to recycle an aluminum can instead of discarding it.

The second challenge is to get someone to not do something they might otherwise do. You might want a smoker to resist the urge to smoke, or you might want a teen to not experiment with drugs.

Sometimes the best way to get people to not do a particular thing is to get them to choose a specific alternative. The best way to get someone to not eat a cookie may be to get him or her at that moment to eat an apple. The best way to get people to not dial 911 when they need nonemergency help may be to get them to dial 311. But sometimes when our goal is to get someone to not do something, the alternative, the "instead of," is not specific. When a young person does not experiment with drugs, there is likely nothing in particular that they do instead. Similarly, when a person does not smoke, there is often nothing in particular that they do as an alternative.

When we seek to stimulate an action whether for its own sake or to replace an action we want to stop, we must deal with the automatic, nonconscious mental system. The automatic system originates impulses to action. It is central to our behavior and should be the focus of most persuasion.

When we seek to prevent an impulse from turning into an action and not replace that original impulse with another, we must deal with the reflective, conscious mental system but not only with the reflective system. The reflective system monitors the impulses suggested by the automatic system and prohibits some from turning into action. When we don't tell someone who is annoying us to "go to hell," our reflective system intercepted that natural impulse. However, our automatic system can aid the deliberate decision not to take an action by linking that action with undesirable associations.

Let's say we seek to prevent angry drivers from giving others "the finger," an action that all too often escalates to violence. The deliberate, conscious mental system performs this task more easily if our automatic system associates someone who gives the finger while driving with the notion of a pathetic loser.[13]

In a related example, a public service campaign by Australia's Road and Traffic Authority sought to reduce speeding. The target was young males. The commercial suggested that men who speed are seen as compensating for small penises. The women in the ad signal their understanding that speeding is directly related to small penis size by raising their little finger.

Whereas the reflective system has to control the impulse, the associations of the automatic system can reduce or increase the power of that impulse. If the automatic system associates speeding with compensation for unfortunate penis size, the job of the deliberate, conscious mental system to rein in the impulse to speed is much easier.

The Australian campaign is an example of an effort to control speeding at the societal level. However, a similar approach will work as well with controlling speeding at the personal level. A passenger might casually comment when observing a speeding driver in another car that the speeding driver is probably trying to compensate for a small penis. After a few such comments, the driver of the passenger's car will likely be careful to avoid speeding himself. The reflective system has to control the impulse to speed, but knowing that the passenger associates speeding with a diminutive penis will make it easier for the deliberate, conscious mental system to rein in the speeding impulse.

The reflective mental system is properly the primary influence in some important, considered decisions. But even when the reflective mental system ultimately makes a decision, the automatic, nonconscious system still plays a large role.

What decision could be more proper for the reflective mental system than deciding whether to have surgery or radiation therapy in treatment of lung cancer? Yet, as Tversky and Kahneman[14] have demonstrated, the words used to describe the risks radically alter the decision. They described the risks in two ways. Half of their respondents saw the options described as follows:

- **Surgery**: Of 100 people having surgery, 90 live through the postoperative period, 68 are alive at the end of the first year, and 34 are alive at the end of five years.

- **Radiation Therapy**: Of 100 people having radiation therapy, all live through the treatment, 77 are alive at the end of one year, and 22 are alive at the end of five years.

The other half saw the exact same options described differently:

- **Surgery**: Of 100 people having surgery, 10 die during surgery or the post-operative period, 32 die by the end of the first year, and 66 die by the end of five years.

- **Radiation Therapy**: Of 100 people having radiation therapy, none die during treatment, 23 die by the end of one year, and 78 die by the end of five years.

In general, people prefer surgery to radiation because surgery results in better long-term survival. However, when the risks are described with different words, even though the risks themselves remain identical, the probability someone will choose radiation changes dramatically.

When the options were presented to subjects in terms of the chances of survival (the first description), 18 percent chose radiation and 82 percent chose surgery.

But when the equivalent options were described in terms of mortality, more than twice as many people chose radiation. In this group, 44 percent chose radiation and 56 percent chose surgery.

The risks were exactly the same in both cases. Only the words used to frame the risks changed. Our automatic system reacts to the words used to frame the risks. The reaction of the lizard inside to the words used to describe the options more than doubled the probability that the reflective system would choose radiation therapy. Incidentally, the size of the effect was the same for business students, clinic patients, and experienced physicians. This means that the influence of the lizard on the decision was the same no matter the decider's level of education or experience.

In order to succeed at persuasion, we have to deal with the lizard inside, the automatic mental system. We have to apply the seven secrets of persuasion:

1. **Speak the language of the lizard.** The nonconscious mind has its own particular method of communication, a language with its own grammar and style.

2. **Aim at the act, not the attitude.** Changing what people do is easier than changing how they feel.

3. **Don't change desires, fulfill them.** Persuasion works by showing people how to get what they want.

4. **Never ask, unearth.** People don't know why they do what they do, but you can find out anyway.

5. **Focus on feeling.** Facts won't alter an emotional choice.

6. **Create experience with expectation.** What people expect to experience transforms what they actually experience.

7. **Add a little art.** Art makes the nonconscious mind your ally.

2

SPEAK THE LANGUAGE OF
THE LIZARD: BASIC GRAMMAR

The language of our reflective, conscious mental system, the mind we know well, is information, logic, and reason. That is why most definitions of persuasion speak of convincing by reasoned argument. But reasoned argument is not the way to persuade the lizard—far from it.

The lizard inside, our automatic, nonconscious mental system, has its own language. As the last 25 years of psychological, behavioral economic, and neurological research has demonstrated, the language of the automatic system has a basic grammar:

- Mental availability.
- Association.

It also has its own style:

- Action.
- Feelings.
- Preferences of others.

Because the lizard is in charge of most of our decisions and influential in the rest, fluency in the language of the lizard is essential to persuasion.

Mental Availability

Daniel Kahneman and Amos Tversky have taught us about the availability heuristic.[1] By that they mean that we nonconsciously use how easily something comes to mind, or mental availability, as a rule of thumb to help us evaluate things and people. Because of the availability heuristic, our automatic system pays the most attention to and assumes the superiority of things and people that spring to mind most easily.

The influence of the ease with which something comes to mind shows up in many aspects of our life and shows up in many areas of the study of human decision-making. Behavioral economists speak of availability and familiarity. Psychologists talk about vividness, salience, anchoring, priming, and mere exposure. Marketers emphasize memorability and repetition. All these concepts are based on this central tendency of our automatic, nonconscious mental system. What springs easily to mind, whether it is people, phrases, ideas, or products, will be more liked, more believed, and more influential in our behavior. Cognitive ease makes us receptive.

When we vote, candidates whose names seem familiar, whether or not they are really familiar, are more likely to get our vote. When making a choice in an unfamiliar category, consumers are more likely to choose the recognized brand even when it is of lesser quality.[2]

A vividly described outcome seems more likely than a blandly described outcome even if the vivid details have no real effect on probability of occurrence. The lizard, our automatic, nonconscious mental system, thinks in terms of vivid stereotypes and exemplars rather than statistics and percentages. That is why an audience is more easily swayed by a surprising individual story than by a surprising statistic.

We worry a lot more about the possibility of being killed by a shark than the possibility of being killed by a falling airplane part. We think more about death by shark attack because it comes more easily to mind. Shark attacks get the attention of the press. The details are vivid and memorable. But, actually, being killed by a falling airplane part is 30 times more likely.[3]

Things that are salient, that is, more prominent or conspicuous, seem to us more significant. A person who is more salient than others in a meeting because of the way she is dressed, because she is sitting under a light, or because of her body language is perceived by us as more influential.[4]

A number mentioned to us, even if we know it was selected randomly, anchors and influences our future numerical estimates of a person's age, the price of an object, or whatever else. Numbers that more easily pop into our mind influence our judgments, even though we know they shouldn't.

Estimates people give of the population of Milwaukee illustrate the power of anchors.[5] People from Chicago consistently overestimate the population of Milwaukee. People from Green Bay consistently underestimate the population of Milwaukee. People from Chicago begin with what they know, the population of Chicago, and adjust downward. People from Green Bay begin with the population of Green Bay and adjust upward. Typically, adjustments are inadequate and the initial anchor has a dramatic effect on the ultimate estimates.

Ideas that have been primed, that is, very subtly suggested to us—so subtly that we aren't even aware they have been suggested—still change our behavior. John Bargh and his colleagues gave us a classic demonstration of the impact of priming. Bargh is a Yale social psychologist who founded Yale's Automaticity in Cognition, Motivation, and Evaluation (ACME) Laboratory. The ACME Laboratory studies the ways in which our environment unconsciously influences how we think, feel, and behave.

Bargh and his colleagues asked college students to create a grammatically correct four-word sentence from each of 30 sets of five words.[6] Half the students were given sets that contained words related to the elderly stereotype like careful, gray, and Florida. The other half of the students were given sets in which neutral words replaced words related to the elderly. After doing this task, the students walked down the hallway to the exiting elevator. The time it took the students to walk down the hallway was secretly measured. The students who had created sentences from the sets of words associated with the elderly walked more slowly. The participants were subtly primed to think of old age. That priming, though nonconscious, had a direct, measureable effect on walking speed.

Robert Zajonc demonstrated more than 40 years ago that "mere exposure" to an arbitrary stimulus (an idea, a thing, or a person) generates "mild affection" for the stimulus.[7] Zajonc spent four decades at the University of Michigan where he was the director of the Institute for Social Research. Zajonc showed that it doesn't seem to matter what the stimulus is. If we have been exposed to a Chinese pictograph, a face, or an irregularly shaped polygon, we feel a little more positively toward it than if we have not been exposed to it. Our mild affection occurs even if we are not consciously aware that we've ever seen the item before.

Repetition and familiarity breed acceptance. As Kahneman said, "A reliable way to make people believe in falsehoods is frequent repetition, because familiarity is not easily distinguished from truth."[8] For the lizard, what comes most easily to mind seems most true. The lizard can't tell the difference between familiarity and accuracy.

Marketers and politicians make great use of the power of repetition. Marketers repeat the same message again and again knowing that, as the message becomes more familiar, it becomes more believable. Politicians place great emphasis on party discipline, ensuring that party members repeat the same talking points in the same phrases again and again knowing that as those phrases become familiar, they begin to have the ring of truth.

Much of persuasion is an attempt to get certain actions to come more easily to mind.

GEICO has taken advantage of the power of mental availability. GEICO is growing rapidly, recently surpassing Allstate to become the number two provider of automobile insurance behind State Farm. GEICO spends more than a billion dollars a year on distinctive, vivid, unexpected, and fun advertising that makes its brand pop into mind when a young person is thinking about automobile insurance.

GEICO sells direct. The primary job of the advertising is to get young prospects to visit Geico.com when thinking about auto insurance. GEICO's mental availability generates Website visits and has fueled its growth.

We often underestimate the dramatic impact mental availability can have on behavior. The utilitarian category of drain cleaners illustrates how a small change in availability can make an unexpectedly big change in what we place in the shopping cart.

Drano is made by S.C. Johnson and Liquid Plumr is made by Clorox. If you are looking for something to help with a clog, both products are likely to be on the shelf. They will be priced about the same. Because either product will be quick to copy any innovation made by the other, both products will have versions that are essentially chemically equivalent. The primary factor that determines choice is mental availability.

Our automatic system pays the most attention to and assumes the superiority of the brand that comes most easily to mind. Because the thing that is clogged is a drain, Drano has the advantage. By its name alone, Drano is the most available drain cleaner option and its dominant market share reflected this fact. People bought more Drano than all other drain cleaners combined.

We at DDB had an idea to increase Liquid Plumr's mental availability and the Clorox company invested in that idea. The idea was simply to get "plumber" to pop into people's heads when they had a clog and to think of Liquid Plumr as "the plumber to call first." The ads featured "real" plumbers who said, "It's not good for us that it

[Liquid Plumr] works, but it does work" and "It's not a big job, but I've got to charge you for coming out there." And, of course, the announcer reminded us that Liquid Plumr is "the plumber to call first."

More people started thinking about plumbers when they had a clog and Liquid Plumr took over category leadership. When availability changed, market share changed.

S.C. Johnson, the manufacturer of Drano, was not about to let this situation continue. S.C. Johnson hired DDB to handle a number of brands, including Drano and, of course, DDB resigned the Liquid Plumr advertising account. Interestingly, S.C. Johnson asked DDB to correct the problem we had created. S.C. Johnson wanted us to reestablish Drano's natural advantage in mental availability. We created an advertising campaign for Drano that placed the focus back on the drain and made sure no plumber was in sight. Our Drano spokesman, wearing a tie, was inside the drain pointing out the muck before Drano application and using the drain as a water slide after Drano application. S.C. Johnson liked the idea and spent behind it. Attention went back on the drain, Drano's mental availability improved, and Drano's market share went back on top.

Drain cleaner wars are essentially mental availability wars. A small change in mental availability can make a big change in market share.

Think of the option you recommend as a rock in the stream of consciousness or, more correctly, the stream of nonconsciousness. If the option is a large enough rock, sufficiently available, the target's thoughts are interrupted by that option which, unbidden, pops into mind. The target won't always choose the option you recommend, but greater availability gives you a much better chance of success.

When you are driving down the road and feeling hungry, McDonald's pops in your head. You might not choose McDonald's, but you have to decide not to.

Adjust accessibility. Make your recommended option more accessible and other options less so.

When we want to help someone, even help ourselves, lose weight, changing the mental availability of the options can be a rather painless approach. If the soft drinks, potato chips, and cookies are put away in the cabinet and what's on the counter, available psychologically and physically, is a bowl of attractive fruit, we influence the outcome. When someone is looking for a snack, fruit won't always be chosen, but by making fruit more mentally available and junk food less available, we've increased the chances that fruit will be picked.

Dr. Brian Wansink is a professor and director of Cornell's Food and Brand Lab. He and his colleagues just completed their Syracuse Study.[9] In the study, they photographed everything in the kitchens of 240 households and weighed the household members. He found that the typical woman who had soft drinks visible anywhere in her kitchen weighed 25 pounds more than her neighbor who didn't have soft drinks visible. He also found that the typical woman who had fruit visible anywhere in her kitchen weighed 13 pounds less than the neighbor who didn't. We can help control our weight by controlling the visibility of the options.

We can change behavior by changing circumstances instead of changing minds. If we make our preferred option more mentally available and make the other options less mentally available, our persuasion will be both more successful and easier to take.

When angling for a raise at work, we can do a few things to increase our mental availability and help our case. The boss will think more highly of and have more confidence in people who come to mind more easily. What can we do to come to mind more easily? We can increase our salience. We can dress a little more conspicuously or arrange our work area a little more distinctively. The expected fades into the background. In meetings we can pick a seat where the light is better, or pick a seat at the end of the table rather than at the side. We can stand when others are sitting or sit when others are standing. Even if we have nothing more to say at the meetings than we normally would, our contribution will feel greater. As a side benefit, everybody at the meeting will pay just a little bit more attention to what we do say.

Set the "anchor" near the desired option.

The boss trying to match us with an appropriate salary is a lot like a person trying to estimate the population of Milwaukee. It's not easy to figure out the right answer. We would like the boss to be thinking about salaries anchored at the higher range analogous to the population of Chicago, rather than the lower range, analogous to the population of Green Bay. Let's say we are working in a moderately sized city and we find information on the salaries of people working at similar positions in New York. The salaries in New York will almost certainly be higher. It wouldn't hurt to pass that information on to the boss even if, when the time comes, we say we realize the cost of living in New York is higher. In any case, we want the boss adjusting down rather than adjusting up, because such adjustments are usually inadequate and we're likely to end up in a better spot.

If we seek donations to a charitable cause, show prospective donors high levels first and let them adjust down. They'll end up in a better place than if we start low.

When offering consumers a product range, we can focus on the high-end version of the brand even though few people may buy that version. Consumers will adjust downward, but they are more likely to end up where we would like.

Let's say you have a new idea, one you'd like your colleagues to get behind. Don't introduce your new idea in complete detail even if you have already worked out the details. Be patient. Name your new idea. Give people a chance to hear the name of the new idea for a few days before you spring the idea on them fully fleshed out. Take advantage of "mere exposure." Hearing the name in advance, even if your colleagues aren't really paying attention, will make them a little more receptive.

Aim for ubiquity. Never miss a chance to get your recommended option in front of your target. People favor the familiar.

If you are trying to help your spouse quit smoking, help him or her keep that quest front and center. Something as simple as small notes that say "Thanks for quitting" stuck in many unexpected places, like dashboards, mirrors, or underwear drawers, can keep the idea top-of-mind and increase chances for success. Better yet, Websites feature long lists of anti-smoking jokes. The jokes may not all be hilarious, but, if found in many, unexpected places, they can keep the idea of quitting close to mind and make success a little more likely.

Yes, the lizard is influenced by mental availability. But sometimes the all-out pursuit of availability causes bizarre and counterproductive attempts at persuasion. In 2004, Quiznos serenaded the brand and its sandwiches in its advertising with a tune from two singing, furry creatures that appeared, for all the world, to be rats or, at least, rat-like. Surely, the ad made the brand come more easily to mind. People were indeed talking about Quiznos's advertising, but they were asking each other, "What were those things?" There are many other ways of being witty, clever, irreverent, and memorable. If the price of mental availability is associating the restaurant and its food with rodents, that price may be too high.

Association

An idea in our mind activates other associated ideas and each of these ideas activates still more ideas, just as words like "gray" and "Florida" activated the idea of elderly people moving slowly in the Bargh experiment. Associations occur even if we don't want them to. We can't stop association. Words call to mind other words, which call to mind memories and emotions and even cause bodily reactions like a smile or a grimace. The bodily reactions in turn reinforce the emotions, making the set of associations mutually reinforcing. This process takes place immediately, effortlessly, and largely outside of our awareness. Most of the ideas activated in our mind never make it to consciousness. The bulk of the work of associative thinking is hidden and nonconscious. We know much less about ourselves than we think we do.[10]

We weave a coherent story about our situation out of the ideas and feelings that association has activated. Ideas that haven't been activated consciously or nonconsciously don't enter into the story and, as a result, don't influence the impressions and impulses that our automatic mental system generates.

Association is a simple and powerful force.

Semioticians (people who study systems of communication) and anthropologists discuss the difference between signs and symbols. The difference is association. A sign has an explicit and specific meaning.

We are all familiar with the sign telling us that smoking is prohibited. The sign carries with it few other associations.

The Statue of Liberty, on the other hand, is a symbol. Ask anyone in the United States what the Statue of Liberty means and they can go on and on. Ask 10 people and you are unlikely to get the same answer twice. The Statue of Liberty calls forth many emotional associations and each associated idea triggers other ideas. A symbol is a concept or figure that has little direct, explicit meaning, but is dense with associated meaning.

Symbols, through the power of association, inspire soldiers to risk their lives, incite religious conflict, and build commercial empires. We are all familiar with the logos of Apple, Nike, and Mercedes. We can see each in our mind's eye and we automatically think of the qualities associated with each.

None of these symbols is powerful because of rational arguments made to the reflective mental system. These symbols derive their power from associations. And associations don't require factual accuracy, just repeated pairings and apparent affiliation. The lizard, the nonconscious mental system, doesn't analyze data. It experiences connections.

I've often wondered why political combatants don't invest more in symbols to help further their policy aims. The set of laws, regulations, and rulings necessary to achieve those policy aims is often complex. But symbols that might represent those policy aims and motivate support could be simple, associational, and emotional. Symbols don't require information or facts. Politicians can spare people that. Symbols require only the shared cultural meaning that is built from repeated poignant connections. Politicians should be better at that.

Let's take Obamacare, Right to Life, and Freedom of Choice as three examples. Each idea is a bundle of rather complex policies. But each idea could be represented by a simple symbol that shortcuts communication, stimulates associations, and stirs emotions. Imagine a shield represents Obamacare (maybe standing for protection against ruinous medical costs). Imagine a seed beginning to sprout represents Right to Life. Imagine an open padlock represents

Freedom of Choice. The specific figure that forms the symbol is not crucial. But the work a persuader does to attach associations to the symbol and give that symbol meaning is critical. The meaning won't be the same for everyone. In fact, the meaning will probably be slightly different for everyone. Each person, at least each fan, can see in the symbol something that is important and motivating to him or her.

All concepts fall along a spectrum of meaning. Symbols, which have vague explicit meaning, but dense associational meaning, are at one end of the spectrum. Signs, which have precise explicit meaning and little associational meaning, are at the other end. Most concepts fall somewhere in between.

Ideas call to mind other ideas. Associations are inevitable. Fortunately, we can influence association. We can direct and enrich the associational meaning of a concept.

In persuasion, we enhance the associations of the behavior we are trying to encourage in a way that makes that behavior more attractive to our target.

Voting can become more appealing through association with other valued concepts like patriotism, power, independence, or fairness. Recycling can become more strongly associated with saving the earth or it can become more strongly associated with government efficiency. These associations can be built at the societal level or at a more personal level within the neighborhood or the family.

A friend once used simple association to persuade his son not to get an earring. He didn't say he objected to the earring, but he cautioned his son about which ear he chose. My friend said he believed that the left ear indicated that the person was straight and the right ear signaled that the person was gay. Or was it the other way around? My friend said he couldn't remember. That was enough. The association of a male earring with an easily misunderstood statement of sexual preference made the thought of an earring a lot less attractive. His son still has no earring.

Marketers and politicians know the power of association doesn't depend on facts, just repeated parings. People infer association from observed juxtapositions.

Indecision is the most common mistake. Whether you are promoting a brand, soliciting donations for a cause, or just trying to get your kids to act differently, explicitly choose the qualities or the sort of people you would like to link to your recommended option. Associations will inevitably occur. You might as well pick the ones you want. Once chosen, repeatedly pair the option with those qualities or with that sort of people. Current factual accuracy is not the issue. You are creating a link, not documenting a link.

NRG Energy is a giant power company. And, according to Forbes, "NRG Energy is one of the nation's biggest operators of carbon-belching power plants."[11] But NRG is developing renewable energy resources and has committed to a 90-percent reduction in its carbon footprint by 2050.

NRG Energy would like to be associated not with the massive amounts of fossil fuels it currently burns, but with the green energy projects it has begun. Rather than wait until green energy becomes a bigger part of their business, NRG Energy would like to be thought of as a green energy company now. To accomplish its goal, NRG uses association in their online video. The video pairs NRG with people choosing a source of power for charging their cell phones—fossil fuel, solar, or wind. The video shows people preferring power sourced from solar and wind and the video goes on to say that NRG is changing its source of power in the same way.

If it follows through with its plans, someday, NRG will be a green energy company. Right now, NRG is not a green energy company. Through association, NRG can become today, in the minds of consumers, the company it hopes to be in the future.

August Busch III, head of Anheuser-Busch, brewer of Budweiser, Bud Light, and Michelob, intuitively understood and feared the power of association.

His competitor, Coors, had been available only west of the Mississippi. For eastern beer drinkers, Coors had the mystique of the inaccessible. When young men drove out West, they would often return with cases of the legendary and impossible-to-find Coors for their friends.

August Busch learned that Coors was planning to roll east of the Mississippi in a couple of years and he was worried about the impact Coors might have on his largest brand, Budweiser. Coors, brewed in Golden, Colorado, was associated with mountains and cowboys. Mountains in turn are associated with attractive ideas like cold, refreshment, nature, and purity. Cowboys call to mind masculinity and independence. Everyone had seen what the connection with cowboys had done for Marlboro. Mountains and cowboys were powerful associations that August Busch did not want to cede to Coors.

His response was to act before Coors rolled eastward and reposition Busch Bavarian Beer to blunt the Coors expansion. Even though Busch Bavarian Beer had no actual connection with the West, August Busch decided to associate Busch with Western mountains and cowboys so Coors would not have those associations all to itself.

Busch Bavarian had been a relatively little used brand in the Anheuser-Busch stable, with limited distribution. In its original incarnation, Busch Bavarian allowed Anheuser-Busch to sell off excess capacity at a discount.

August Busch dropped "Bavarian," changing the name of the beer from "Busch Bavarian" to simply "Busch." He had the can and label redesigned. Busch Bavarian graphics had featured the Alps. August Busch wanted the mountains on the label and can to look more like the Rockies.

When he met with the Busch brand team and us, the agency, August Busch insisted that all ads for Busch Beer contain three elements: cowboys, mountains, and the line "Head for the Mountains."

August Busch broadened distribution of Busch Beer to cover the entire area of the Coors intended expansion.

In advance of the Coors expansion, Busch held "Mountain Man" promotions and hired Hoyt Axton to sing "Head for the mountains, the mountains of Busch."

Coors still rolled eastward with some success, but its success was mitigated. As intended, Busch Beer muddied the Coors association with mountains and cowboys.

One of my first assignments in advertising was to answer a question about association. It came from the brand manager of Busch Beer. At that time, every ad featured a bit of a set up followed by the opening of a can of Busch. The sound made when the can was opened, with the help of the sound track, was an exaggeration of the brand name, "Busssssch." At that sound, the advertising cut to an animal in the snow turning its head as if reacting to the can opening. The idea being that the opening of a can of Busch marked the transition from whatever you were doing to cold, mountain refreshment. The brand manager wanted to know which animals to use for the "head turn." He felt the animal used should be associated with masculinity, because everything about the ad had to reflect the masculine image of the brand he was trying to create.

After some investigation in the literature and with consumers, I remember reporting that the gender of the animal was not what was most important in communicating masculinity. All an animal needs to communicate masculinity is size and aggressiveness. Large, aggressive animals are seen as masculine. Smaller, less-aggressive animals are seen as feminine. From that time on, the response to the can opening featured a horse rearing up in the snow. The horse had three things going for it. It was large. In rearing, it was aggressive. And, of course, a horse fits with cowboys.

Spirit Airline provides an example of an advertiser failing to take into account the associations that can sink its message. A big chunk of Spirit Airline's business is flying people back and forth between where they normally live and sunny Florida. The massive BP oil spill in the Gulf in 2010 made many people rethink their Florida vacation. Spirit had a big idea: remind people that everything they like about Florida is still true of the Atlantic coast. Their ads promoted travel to Ft. Lauderdale with a photo of a beautiful woman in a bikini, slathered with sun tan lotion lying on the beach under the headline, "Check out the oil on our beaches." In attracting people to Florida, did Spirit Airlines really want to reinforce an association between Florida beaches and oil? With a little work, the viewer understands the oil referred to is sun tan oil, not spilled crude. Encouraging people to dig a little deeper to understand an ad can be effective when the first meaning that comes to mind doesn't make sense. But when the first meaning that comes to mind does make sense, spilled oil on beaches, people will look no further. The ads were clever, yes, but too clever.

Brand associations are powerful for good or for ill.

3

SPEAK THE LANGUAGE OF
THE LIZARD: STYLE

A persuader can also use the style of the lizard's language—action, emotion, and the preferences of others. Important as these three are in influencing the automatic system, they typically work through availability and association. Action, emotion, and the preferences of others can increase the mental availability of an option and modify its associations.

Action

We have all been told that actions speak louder than words. Certainly that's the case for the lizard. Observers of a social scene pay close attention to the actions of participants, not their motivations. Research has shown that observers will judge the character of the participants on the basis of their actions alone, largely ignoring the constraints of the situation. Even if participants could hardly have acted any other way, observers will judge the participants by their actions. If a law student is assigned to defend a racist point of view, a point of view that observers know the law student does not hold, his defense of that point of view will still color observers' opinion of him. This phenomenon is part of what psychologists call "the fundamental attribution error."[1]

Marketers often make use of the fundamental attribution error, though they don't call it that.

Abercrombie & Fitch was for many years a high-end brand of sporting goods and apparel—hunting and fishing in particular. In the late 1980s, The Limited bought Abercrombie & Fitch. The Limited decided to use the brand to sell apparel to young people. The Limited wanted to make Abercrombie & Fitch fashionable. How does an upscale but dated brand of sporting goods become a fashionable brand?

The Limited changed perceptions of Abercrombie & Fitch by changing the way the brand acted. No internal brand personality determined what Abercrombie & Fitch did. Brands do what they do not because of who they are, but because of who they want to become. And who each brand wants to become, of course, is a brand that makes a lot of money. The brand acted fashionably in its daring catalogue, in the media, and in the store and we observers came to see Abercrombie & Fitch as inherently fashionable despite the obvious profit motive for its behavior. For the lizard, "Behavior engulfs the field."[2] In other words, for the lizard, you are what you do no matter why you do it.

Abercrombie & Fitch couldn't become fashionable in the eyes of potential buyers by *claiming* to be fashionable. No brand can effectively claim to be fashionable. Nor can a brand successfully claim to be fun, exciting, or manly. A brand can't argue its way to those perceptions. In order to become perceived as fashionable, fun, exciting, or manly, a brand has to act fashionably, fun, exciting, or manly. People will ignore the constraints of marketing and profit. People will judge the brand on its action.

The Apple ad for its MacBook featuring 74 different MacBook decals didn't claim that the brand or its users are fun, confident, creative, and cool. The ad just had to act that way and viewers got the message. Viewers get much more information about the brand and its users by how a message acts than by what the message literally says.

An oil company can create an image for itself as environmentally conscious by its actions. The oil company may not be environmentally conscious at all, but its actions can convince people of its environmental concern. The oil company can donate to the Audubon Society. It can speak in favor of higher mileage requirements for cars. It can paint its gas stations green. This will likely cause people to think the oil company is environmentally conscious even though the real reason for its behavior may be to get offshore drilling licenses. You are what you do no matter why you do it.

How would your candidate act if he or she were indeed compassionate, tough, honest, or open-minded? Act that way and he or she will be perceived that way and no one will question the motivation. Even a milquetoast brand can be seen as rugged if it acts ruggedly. Your option and the people who seem to choose it will be believed to be the way they act no matter why they act that way.

Belvedere Vodka provides another, but an unfortunate, example of the impact of action on perception. Belvedere's slogan was "Always goes down smoothly." So far so good. However, in their Facebook and Twitter ads, Belvedere superimposed this slogan over a photo of a young man with a smile on his face forcibly restraining a young woman who seems desperate to get away. Above the photo, in smaller type of a different color, the copy read, "unlike some people." A casual reader sees Belvedere making a connection between what looks like attempted rape and the brand. Why the brand made this connection is largely irrelevant; the action looks to be attempted rape. For the lizard, you are what you do no matter why you do it.

Of course, Belvedere Vodka apologized, but the lizard pays attention to action, not apologies.

Parents instinctively use action to persuade toddlers to eat what's good for them. Dealing with the lizard inside an adult is a lot like dealing with a toddler. Parents don't try to explain to the toddler that the food is enjoyable. They know the toddler wouldn't be convinced. Parents show the toddler that they themselves enjoy the food by eating some with obvious pleasure. They know that toddlers still won't always be convinced, but they also know that action has a much better chance of persuading than explanation.

Mark Twain understood this.

Discouraged, Tom Sawyer sat down facing "the far-reaching continent of unwhitewashed fence." Aunt Polly wanted the fence whitewashed, and it looked to Tom like he had no way out. He wanted his friends to take over the job, but when he examined his pockets for toys and trash, he saw "not half enough to buy so much as half an hour of pure freedom."[3] However, Tom had an inspiration. He would persuade his friends not with barter, but with action. Tom began to act as if he enjoyed whitewashing the fence and as if he took great pride in the finished appearance. Soon, rather than laughing at his predicament, Tom's friends were lining up for a chance to take a turn at whitewashing.

"Behavior engulfs the field." Toddlers don't question their parents' real motives for acting like they enjoy the food. Tom's fictional friends didn't question his real motives for acting like he enjoyed whitewashing the fence.

Action communicates with the lizard and the lizard ignores the motive behind the action.

Reciprocity serves as an entirely different illustration of the impact a person's actions have on our judgment. Robert Cialdini of Arizona State University observed successful compliance practitioners 30 years ago. He identified reciprocity as one of the tactics they employ.[4] When someone is nice to us, we feel kindly toward them even if, when we think about it, we realize their action is motivated by profit, not affection. Reciprocity is special because we not only pay attention to the behavior and ignore the motive, we feel obligated to be nice in return.

Human relationships are largely built by social exchange and reciprocity is the basis of social exchange. Social exchange is best understood in contrast to economic exchange.

Economic exchange, such as purchasing something for money in a grocery store, is precise and immediate. The checker totals up how much we owe to the penny. We pay without delay. And we leave with no debt and feeling no obligation to the store, its manager, or its personnel. Economic exchange does not lead to a relationship. In fact, it is designed to avoid building a relationship.

But social exchange, for example a dinner invitation followed by a reciprocal invitation, is imprecise and often delayed. Social exchange is designed to create a relationship. The obligation we feel to reciprocate builds the relationship.

We are preprogrammed to feel this obligation to reciprocate. It is built into our automatic, nonconscious mental system. Even if we consciously recognize manipulation, we still have an impulse to reciprocate. That is why a rug merchant in Istanbul will always offer complimentary tea before displaying his wares. We know the offer of tea is a sales tool, but accepting the merchant's tea still makes us far more likely to reciprocate by at least listening politely to his sales pitch.

Emotion

Our automatic system responds to emotion because the automatic system itself uses emotion—liking, repulsion, fear, happiness—to communicate its desires.

Researchers have extensively explored the impact of liking, or what psychologists call the "affect heuristic."[5] If we like an idea, a thing, or a person, we assume it possesses an abundance of positive qualities and a minimum of negative qualities, even if we don't have good evidence one way or the other. Similarly, if we dislike an idea, thing, or person, we assume it possesses an abundance of negative qualities and a minimum of positive ones.[6] As a result, we tend to see the world as much simpler and more coherent than it actually is. In the real world, ideas, things, and people tend to have both positive and negative qualities, but our feelings bias the way we perceive these qualities.

People on different sides of an issue have a difficult time talking to each other because of the affect heuristic. Rather than looking objectively at all the evidence, we tend to notice evidence that reinforces our pre-existing feelings. When we feel positively about a particular politician, we pay close attention to information that puts him or her in a good light. If we feel negatively about that politician, we pay close attention to information that puts him or her in a bad light. As Daniel Kahneman tells us, "Our comforting conviction that the world makes sense rests on a secure foundation: our almost unlimited ability to ignore our ignorance."[7]

Pampers has put the affect heuristic to good use. The brand produced a beautiful, emotional, video lullaby. A mother softly sings to her baby while charming, multi-national scenes of people making life "better for baby" illustrate her lyrics.

Why did Pampers create this video? Is the Pampers brand, in fact, warm and caring and willing to do anything to make life "better for baby"? Maybe.

Pampers is also part of a giant, worldwide, consumer products corporation with more than $80 billion in sales last year. Pampers has profit demands like every brand in P&G. Pampers is probably genuinely concerned with the welfare of babies. Surely, that is good business. On the other hand, a genuine concern for the welfare of babies is not why this video was created.

This emotional video influences our perception of Pampers. It doesn't matter that the decision to create the video was calculated and can be justified to the corporation as improving the bottom line. It doesn't matter that the video was done so that when people stand in the baby supplies section of their store, the emotional experience of this video will give them a little nudge in the Pampers' direction.

Some may feel that the video is manipulative. It is. Its music and images were skillfully combined to evoke viewers' emotion. That doesn't matter. The video is an example of creativity and emotion harnessed to build a brand and make a profit.

Classic Hallmark ads are another good example of the use of emotion in persuasion. Everyone is familiar with the format. Whether it's a husband giving a card to his wife, a child giving a card to a parent, or a grandchild giving a card to an aging grandparent, we know what to expect. Hallmark uses emotion to speak to the lizard and we end up fighting a tear. For the lizard, feeling the emotion is what's important. Why or how Hallmark made us feel that way doesn't matter.

Hallmark uses the ads as a sampling program, providing millions of people a small sample of the emotional experience of giving someone a Hallmark card. We come to associate that emotional reward with Hallmark. The company effectively uses emotion to speak to the lizard and, as a result, earns remarkable profits on cardboard, ink, and creative talent. Greeting cards may be declining in popularity, but that is because of a communication revolution outside Hallmark's control.

Thinking of persuasion as a sampling program can often be useful. Whether we would like someone to stop smoking or go on a date with us, consider whether the message itself can provide a small sample of the emotional experience the target might expect from doing what we ask. Can the children host a small celebration in honor of dad's decision to quit smoking, providing him a sample of the affection and gratitude he can expect from continuing to not smoke? When a young man invites a young woman on a date, can he make the invitation itself charming and amusing, providing a small sample of what the date itself might be like?

Emotional associations are better remembered. When you pair your recommended option with a quality or a person, help the target feel warm, happy, angry, or amused at the same time, the link will endure.

Sometimes attempts to reach the lizard through the use of emotion backfire. The famous Schlitz campaign, popularly known as the "Drink Schlitz or I'll kill you" campaign, is a case in point. This campaign dates back to the time when Schlitz was a beer brand to take seriously. Each ad featured a tough man, for example a boxer or a Hell's Angel's type. The man was asked to switch from Schlitz to another brand of beer. He aggressively refused to give up his Schlitz and threatened anyone who would try to take it away from him. The ads were over the top, surely not meant to be taken seriously.

But people responded to the campaign, not by thinking logically that manly men really like Schlitz, and not with the emotion of liking the beer as Schlitz had hoped. Viewers responded with the emotion of fear. The ads actually communicated that Schlitz and people who like Schlitz are frightening. This campaign and several other marketing missteps led to Schlitz's precipitous downfall.

The Preferences of Others

The power of the influence of others on our choices seems to lie deep in our evolutionary past. We, like many animals, copy.

The copying instinct may be most visible in mating habits. Scientists have seen that a male becomes more appealing as a mating prospect if other females have already selected him as a mate.[8]

Consider the lek. A lek is a gathering of males engaged in competitive display that plays a large role in the mating habits of several species. During breeding season, males in these species gather together, each in his own small, delineated territory where he can show off for visiting females. Females wander through this display area and eventually mate with one of the males. Typically, a few of the males attract most of the females.

Scientists have studied leks to better understand how the process works. A male's mating success seems to depend not just on his own appearance and performance, but also on females copying each other. Females are more attracted to males that have other females close by.[9] Sage grouse hens are more likely to choose to mate with a male if other females have already chosen him. The likelihood of a female fallow deer or sage grouse entering the territory of a male is positively associated with the number of females already present. In a particularly clever experiment, scientists found that placing a stuffed female black grouse in the territory of a male who had failed to mate resulted in an increase in the number of females who enter that luckless male's territory. Females are influenced by the preferences of other females.

At the human level as well, our automatic, nonconscious mental system uses the preferences of others to help us form our own preferences and even to help us evaluate how happy we are with a choice we have already made.

At our advertising agency, we would, for any brand, divide buyers of its product category into groups. Let's take Nike for example. Consumers who buy athletic shoes generally know Nike. We call these consumers Nike Acquaintances. Among Acquaintances, some would consider buying Nike. These are Friends of Nike. Among Friends, some definitely plan to buy Nike and describe Nike as one of their favorites. These are Nike Lovers.

The concentric circles that follow illustrate the relationship between Acquaintances, Friends, and Lovers.

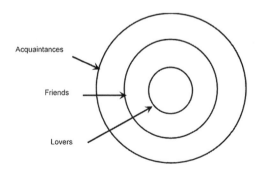

Many people expect that a brand with a very wide circle of Friends would have a relatively low proportion of Lovers among those Friends. The thinking is that a brand that has made itself acceptable to most category users must have rounded off its edges and become bland. Similarly, many people expect that, if a brand has a smaller circle of Friends, it would have a higher proportion of Lovers among those Friends because the brand had been true to a sharply defined identity. Those few Friends must see something uniquely attractive in it.

We noticed a very different pattern. Around the world and across product categories, when a brand has more Friends, a higher proportion of those Friends are Lovers. The pattern is the same for sports apparel brands in China, camera brands in Germany, and tire brands in the United States.

In China, about 22 percent of the population would consider buying Fila; that is, 22 percent of the Chinese population are Fila Friends. And about 10 percent of those Fila Friends say they would definitely buy Fila and that Fila is one of their favorites; that is, 10 percent of Fila Friends are Fila Lovers. On the other hand, about 62 percent of the Chinese population are Nike Friends. And about 19 percent of those Friends are Nike Lovers. Nike not only has many more Friends than Fila, but each of those Friends is almost twice as likely to be a Nike Lover.

If a brand has a lot of Friends, a lot of those many Friends are Lovers. If a brand has few Friends, few of those few Friends are Lovers. The pattern holds for most any category around the world. Depth of affection grows along with breadth of popularity. The feelings of all influence the affection of each. The preferences of others influence our preferences.

Andrew Ehrenberg and his colleagues have repeatedly demonstrated the practical implications of this phenomenon in buying behavior, a pattern they call "Double Jeopardy."[10] They look at brand penetration—the proportion of the population who buys the brand at least once in a time period (usually a year), and brand frequency—the average number of times the brand was purchased in the period by each of those who purchased it at all. They found that brands with higher penetration had consistently higher frequency. When more people bought a brand at all, those buyers bought that brand with greater average frequency. They found this same pattern across categories around the world.

The relationship of Lovers to Friends and the relationship of frequency of purchase to penetration illustrate the impact that the preferences of others have on how we feel and act. If a brand has a lot of Friends, each of those Friends is more likely to be a Lover. If a brand has more buyers, those buyers buy the brand more often.

To appeal to a broader range of customers, a brand need not, in fact shouldn't, dull its distinctiveness. A great brand focuses clearly and precisely on something that many people want, and works to be better at providing that than any other brand. Everybody wants to feel like an athlete. Nike and Gatorade are better than other brands at allowing everyone to feel that way. If Nike or Gatorade watered down their athletic drive, everyone would feel shortchanged.

Laughter yoga provides a good illustration of the ability of the behavior of others to influence our behavior. According to *Time* magazine, there are more than 400 laughter yoga clubs in the U.S.[11] In a laughter yoga session, a group of people gather together in a room, look at each other, and simulate laughing. No jokes and no humorous material are used. In fact, such material is discouraged. Soon, without the benefit of any amusing stimulus, simulated laughter turns into real laughter for some and quickly the real laughter is infectious for all. A room full of people who were not laughing becomes a room full of people who are heartily laughing through a process that completely bypasses conscious thought. Proponents of laughter yoga claim all sorts of health benefits. The health benefits may or may not exist. But it is clear that the laughter of others can cause us to laugh even if we know that those others are not laughing at anything in particular.

Social scientists remind us that we are preprogrammed to imitate.[12] Social perception automatically results in corresponding social behavior. When we see someone yawn, we start to yawn as well. When we see someone scratch his head, we do so too. When we see elderly people, we start to walk more slowly and we become a bit forgetful.

We don't decide to imitate. Like fish, we automatically behave like those around us.

Some social scientists feel that social influence works because we use the preferences of others to guide our choices. They say we assess an object's value by both what we ourselves personally know of that object and by the value we see others place in it. These scientists speak of "information cascades."[13] An "information cascade" begins when what we learn from others about the value of an object outweighs whatever personal experience we have. Because we can't know everything about every object, it is only natural that we would pay attention to how others feel. The logic of online sites like TripAdvisor reflects this reality. Five-star reviews by thousands of raters are remarkably persuasive.

In experiments with music sharing, Salgonic, Dodds, and Watts saw the effect of information cascades.[14] They divided participants in their music-sharing experiments into random groups. They found that the early downloads of people in each group had a dramatic impact on the music that became favored by the whole of each group. Early downloads revealed the value others placed on specific music.

Early actors have an inordinate influence on the behavior of later actors. If you are one of the first to speak at a parent-teacher meeting, you can influence the tone of the whole meeting by making a polite comment or an angry comment. If you are seated toward the front of a theater and you quickly jump to your feet to applaud at the end of a performance, you will dramatically raise the likelihood of a standing ovation from the whole audience.

One of the easiest ways to influence the behavior of others is to prominently act the way you would like them to act. Give your seat to an elderly person on the bus and others will also. Make it clear you are not drinking because you are driving and others are likely to join you in your abstinence. Don't underestimate the urge to imitate.

We see the power of the tendency to imitate in the persuasive technique of "scarcity."[15] Items for sale become more attractive to us if there appear to be only a few left. What is motivating to us are not the few left, but the many that have already been sold. If only a few remain, we are limited in our ability to imitate the many people who have already purchased, and this gives some urgency to our own purchase. If there are only a few left, but there were only a few to begin with, the scarcity doesn't motivate us.

If you are or have been the parent of a teen, your teen no doubt has said they want to do something "because everybody's doing it." In response you probably heard yourself say, "If everybody jumps in the lake, are you going to jump in the lake too?" The influence of the preferences of others is particularly strong among teens and the others they are most concerned with are peers, not family.

Advertisers of course know about the influence of the preferences of others. That's why ads of all sorts attempt to tap into that power with claims of "America's favorite" or "More people choose…." Even if marketers can't make such a claim, they use marketing to create the impression of popularity because they know the power of our perception of the preferences of others.

We discovered that the impact of the preferences of others on us is particularly strong if we believe the number of people who feel that preference is growing. If we believe both that a lot of people recycle and that the number of people who recycle is growing, we are more likely to recycle ourselves. If we believe a lot of people recycle, but we believe the number of people who recycle is declining, we are not as motivated to recycle. It seems that the lizard responds to not just the preferences of others today, but what it senses the preferences of others are going to be tomorrow.

To harness the power of the preferences of others, promise to provide what most of those others want. A brand should promise to fulfill a desire that is one of the fundamental motivations for using the category, a desire that is felt by most category users. You can then go on to explain why your brand's way of fulfilling that desire is superior to other ways of fulfilling that desire. If your brand is an athletic shoe, promise to satisfy one of the fundamental motivations for buying athletic shoes and tell us why your way of satisfying that motivation is better. If your brand is a drain cleaner, promise to satisfy one of the fundamental motivations people have for buying a drain cleaner and tell us why your way of satisfying that motivation is better. Success in marketing follows from being perceived as uniquely able to provide something many people want.

Popularity and momentum are hard to resist. People will value your option if it seems to be popular and/or growing more popular. Even affection depends on popularity. Forget the appeal of the lone wolf unless everybody wants to follow the lone wolf's path. People's imitation of those around them is automatic. Point out and play up fellow travelers.

Though marketers often try to tap into the influence of the preferences of others, they sometimes run afoul of this "popularity principle" because of an exaggerated belief in the power of segmentation. The most common form of segmentation identifies groups within the marketer's target population that show different patterns of desires. Typically, many desires, and usually the most fundamental desires, are common across all groups within a target. However, segmentation takes the focus off common desires and places the focus on minor differences in the pattern of desire.

When a segmentation study selects the reward to associate with the brand, commonly felt desires are likely to be ignored in favor of minor differences in desire. Segmentation studies, when done right, can be useful in secondary marketing to groups within the overall target, but segmentation studies are not appropriate for finding the one reward that will motivate the bulk of the target.

Consider the choice you have to make about where to get an oil change, new brakes, a new muffler, new shock absorbers, new tires, or whatever when you are not taking your car to the new car dealer. In other words, consider the consumer decision about auto aftermarket service. Midas asked people what was important in their choice. Some people said they put most emphasis on dealing with a local mechanic that they knew. Other people said they put more emphasis on price. Still others said they put more emphasis on the expected quality of the parts. This pattern continued with each group of people saying they put a little more emphasis than other people on one thing or another. By the time Midas was done, they had identified 13 different segments in the population, each segment saying what was important in their choice was slightly different from what the other segments said was important.

This analysis of the auto aftermarket decision was unfortunate for two reasons.

First, strange as it seems, people don't know how they decide or what is important in their choice. You can find out what you need to know, but you won't find out by asking. Chapter 6, "Never Ask, Unearth," explains how this works.

Second, the segmentation technique took the emphasis off the most fundamental desires felt commonly across the population and put the emphasis on minor differences in the pattern of desire. Midas is an enormous company doing business with a broad cross section of the population. No one of those identified segments contained even a third of past Midas customers or a third of those people who thought they might be Midas customers in the near future. The segmentation study provided little general direction for Midas marketing.

Surely people choose Midas because they feel Midas offers the best combination of many factors like its neighborhood location, its prices, the quality of its parts, the quality of the mechanic's work, and so forth. Picking any one of those factors or even a narrow set of those factors as Midas's marketing's focus would probably be a mistake. Midas needed to emphasize some more general desire that implied high performance on a broad range of those more narrow factors—something like "Midas is the choice of people who really know cars" because car experts would of course choose someplace that offered the best combination of quality of service, quality of parts, and price. Or Midas could emphasize the trustworthiness of the Midas man, implying quality, price, and fairness, allaying people's fear of being ripped off in car repair.

As a colleague, Ned Anschuetz, advised, marketers should segment supply not demand. By that he meant that marketers should emphasize what makes their brand different from and superior to other sources of supply, but should emphasize what makes their brand the right choice for anyone who feels the need. To be successful, a brand should become perceived as uniquely able to provide something many people want.

Marketers become so involved in this segmentation mindset that they sometimes think an effective way to convince group A that they want a product is to convince them that group B rejects it. We've all seen attempts to convince the young of the desirability of a course of action by convincing them that the old don't understand and certainly don't desire that course of action. It's the marketing version of the political idea that my enemy's enemy must be my friend. If I'm young and old people reject a course of action, then I should embrace that course of action. But in marketing, different groups are not enemies. They are just a little different.

The short life of McDonald's Arch Deluxe line of products illustrates the mistake marketers sometimes make in dealing with the lizard's tendency to pay attention to the preferences of others. McDonald's was unhappy with its kid-centered reputation. They felt they could increase business with Arch Deluxe, a line of products designed specifically to appeal to adults. As a shortcut to communicating that adults like Arch Deluxe products, McDonald's decided to communicate that kids do not like Arch Deluxe products. The ads featured children grimacing at the sight and description of an Arch Deluxe sandwich. The short cut led into a swamp.

Think of all the foods that kids like that adults also like (ice cream, french fries, hot dogs, popcorn, cherries) and all the foods that kids dislike that most adults also dislike (Limburger cheese, castor oil, liver). Kid disapproval doesn't imply adult approval. If anything, when kids dislike the taste of something, adults are understandably wary. The preferences of others, even if the others are children and I am an adult, influence my preferences. The Arch Deluxe was a marketing disaster.

McDonald's subsequently realized that it did not need to worry about whether it was a children's restaurant or an adult restaurant. The McDonald's target is universal. McDonald's does segment the market, but very differently from the usual market segmentation. McDonald's realized its target shouldn't be a specific group of people; rather, its target should be a specific facet of every person. McDonald's is a restaurant for the child in everyone.

When we wish to persuade parents to make more healthful choices in the grocery store, logic will likely have little effect. We need to speak the language of the lizard.

Can we, for example, make more healthful choices more available—that is, more physically or psychologically salient in the store?

Can we adjust the automatic associations that spring into parents' minds when thinking about more healthful choices? Can we associate more healthful choices, not with boring compromise, but with interesting experience; not with feelings of denial, but with feelings of being a good parent?

Any communication about more healthful choices will be seen as the action of those more healthful choices. A dull, tedious message will tell parents and kids that those choices are themselves dull and tedious. An interesting message will tell parents and kids that more healthful choices are themselves interesting. The message will be seen as an action of the more healthful choices that will over-whelm other perceptions.

Can we increase, even a little, the affection people feel for those more healthful choices? Just getting healthful choices to spring more easily to mind will increase parents' affection for them.

Can we get parents to sense the growing popularity of those more healthful choices, in effect encouraging parents to get on board?

Our reflective, conscious mental system monitors the impressions and impulses of the automatic system. Usually our reflective system is content to lay back and go along with what the automatic system suggests. But occasionally, like when we are about to tell someone to "Go to hell," the reflective system engages and forces the consideration of other courses of action.

Our reflective, conscious mental system requires focused attention and responds to evidence and reasoned argument. Persuasion that seeks to influence our reflective mental system can be thought of as following an informational or educational model of persuasion. Facts and logic are critical. However, our automatic system never relaxes and always plays an important role making any impulse more or less appealing. We probably place too much faith in the power of the informational approach to persuasion.

The attempt to influence buying prepared food in New York City is a good example of mistaken faith in the informational approach. Obesity is a growing societal problem. More and more food is consumed out-of-home, and these food choices are believed to be contributing to the obesity problem. People are choosing high-calorie options when lower-calorie options are available. Authorities in New York City decided to do something about it. The problem, they felt, was lack of information. In 2008, the city of New York required any restaurant chain with 20 or more outlets to post the calories of all options as prominently as the price. This is a massive, natural experiment. Thousands and thousands of restaurants dramatically increased the information they provide to millions of consumers across many millions of buying occasions.

What was the impact on buying behavior? Nothing.

Christine Johnson, director of Nutrition Policy, Cardiovascular Disease Prevention and Control Program, NYC Department of Health and Mental Hygiene, told a committee of the National Institute of Health on October 25, 2010, that restaurant patrons showed no evidence of a reduction in calories purchased after the introduction of the law. Elbel, et al. (2009) reached a similar conclusion. People bought just as many calories after the new law as they bought before the new law.[16]

We need to deal with who is in charge. With out-of-home food choices, as with many daily decisions, the automatic system, the lizard, is in charge. The reflective system is not in charge and factual information is not the answer. Rational information can have little impact on a decision that is not rationally made.

Even in the world of advertising, the rational model of the mind has long held sway. Advertisers in general and advertising testers in particular assumed the validity of a rational, linear hierarchy of effects process of persuasion. Many different hierarchies have been proposed.[17] Probably the most popular hierarchy was AIDA for Awareness, Interest, Desire, Action. What all hierarchies had in common was the conviction that persuasion consisted of an orderly, linear flow from information to attitude to behavior. Gifted creators of persuasive messages knew instinctively that persuasion often didn't work that way. The conflict between the two notions of how advertising worked led to many years of tension in advertising development.

At last, things may be starting to change, as evidenced by recent articles in *The International Journal of Market Research* and the *Journal of Advertising Research*. "Fifty Years Using the Wrong Model of Advertising" is the title of an article by Dr. Robert Heath and Paul Feldwick in *The International Journal of Market Research*.

"How Emotional Tugs Trump Rational Pushes: The Time Has Come to Abandon a 100-Year Old Advertising Model" is the title of an article by Orlando Wood in the *Journal of Advertising Research*. Both articles contrast the linear, rational model of decision-making with the automatic, nonconscious model of decision-making revealed by recent psychological, behavioral economic, and neuroscience research, and intuitively understood by gifted persuaders.

Both articles discuss the fact that the linear, rational model makes testing easier. One can easily measure whether people are consciously aware of the message, can repeat some content of the message, and have changed their conscious intention to choose the subject brand. Because most choices don't work in this rational, linear way, such measurements are reminiscent of the drunk looking for his keys under the lamppost, not because that is where he lost them, but because that's where the light's good.

Why did the rational model of the mind so long dominate our thinking and our science even though our most important decisions, such as choice of spouse, or religion, or friends, are clearly not based on a rational consideration of pros and cons? Why do most definitions of persuasion speak of convincing by means of reasoned argument when most of our decisions are not reasoned decisions?

The rational model persists because decision-making *feels* rational.

We are simply not aware of the forces at work outside of consciousness. We don't realize we make many of our decisions before we become conscious we have made them.

Benjamin Libet was a scientist and researcher at the University of California, San Francisco, who did groundbreaking work in the study of human consciousness. He was honored for "pioneering achievements in the experimental investigation of consciousness, initiation of action, and free will." Libet and his colleagues demonstrated in 1983 that we consciously "decide" to act about 200 milliseconds (two tenths of a second) before acting.[18] However, we have an unconscious impulse to act about 500 milliseconds before acting—that is, about 300 milliseconds before we consciously "decide" to act. This unconscious impulse likely causes both "deciding" to act and acting.

In a remarkable experiment in 2008 at the Max Planck Institute for Human Cognitive and Brain Science in Leipzig, Germany, the team led by John-Dylan Haynes also looked at the timing of nonconscious and conscious decision-making.[19] Haynes's results were even more dramatic than Libet's.

Haynes and his colleagues had people decide if they wanted to press a button with their left or right hand. The experiment was set up so subjects could remember at what time they felt their decision was made. The scientists recorded brain activity in the time before subjects felt the decision was made. The scientists found that nonconscious brain activity up to seven seconds before the decision was consciously made could predict whether subjects would press the button with their left or right hand. The scientists knew what the participant was going to do before the participant was conscious of the decision.

Timothy Wilson is a cognitive psychologist at the University of Virginia who studies the influence of our unconscious mind on how we think, choose, and act. Wilson describes the situation like this: "We often experience a thought followed by an action, and assume it was the thought that caused that action. In fact, a third variable, a nonconscious intention, might have produced both the conscious thought and the action."[20]

Some ask if the Haynes findings and the Libet findings call our free will into question. Dr. Haynes responds that the decisions were indeed freely made by the brain, just not by the conscious mind.

The lizard is in charge and we need to use the language the lizard understands—availability, association, action, emotion, and the preferences of others. In most decisions, reason plays a minor role.

When a decision is not made rationally, reasons are unlikely to change it.

4

AIM AT THE ACT,
NOT THE ATTITUDE

Scholars have said attitude is the key target of persuasion.[1] Persuasion attempts are indeed often designed to change our attitude toward a candidate, toward smoking, toward buying healthier foods, toward brand A, or toward our pro-life or pro-choice point of view.

But attitude shouldn't be the key target of persuasion.

The real goal of persuasion is to change behavior—to get someone to act differently, to get a voter to vote for your candidate, to get a smoker to stop smoking, to get a parent to buy healthier foods for the family, to get a shopper to choose brand A over brand B, or to get a legislator to take action in keeping with your pro-life or pro-choice agenda.

If you succeed in getting someone to act the way you want, your persuasion attempt succeeds whether or not attitudes change. If you fail to get someone to act the way you want, your persuasion attempt fails whether or not attitudes change.

Imagine you are working for a major metropolitan city government. Like many cities, yours has overcrowded roadways and a mass transportation system that is losing money because of declining ridership. The mayor asks you to get some people off the roadways and onto mass transportation, easing both problems at once. With enormous effort and expense, you put together a communication campaign that generates a more negative attitude toward driving to work and a more positive attitude toward commuting by mass transit. If, despite the effort and the attitude change, people are still overcrowding the roadways and avoiding mass transit, your work has been in vain and the mayor will not be pleased. On the other hand, you might put your effort into making parking at city lots downtown a little more expensive and using the additional money to make mass transit a little less expensive. With this approach, you may have success at getting some drivers out of their cars and on to mass transit without necessarily changing attitudes. In the first case you have gotten attitude change without behavior change. In the second, you have gotten behavior change without attitude change. I suspect the mayor would be happier with the latter.

Attitude change is one possible way of getting someone to act differently. But attitude change is not the only way and is quite likely not the most effective way.

We often choose attitude change as the goal of persuasion because it feels so good when someone else comes to agree with our view of the world. Goethe observed, "People have a peculiar pleasure in making converts, that is, in causing others to enjoy what they enjoy, thus finding their own likeness represented and reflected back to them."[2] In fact, Goethe felt that "[t]o make converts is the natural ambition of everyone." We know how good it would feel to get someone to agree with us and we aim for that feeling.

A second reason we make attitude change as the goal of persuasion is because it is hard to imagine a change in behavior happening in any other way. Even social scientists have had trouble imagining a change in behavior before a change in attitude. When attitude research was in its infancy, scientists assumed that human behavior is guided by attitudes.[3] If attitude guides behavior, the thinking went, we should be able to change behavior by changing attitude.

But it turned out that the connection between attitudes and behavior was weak.

In an influential review of 47 studies of the relationship between attitudes and behavior, Allan Wicker found that the assumed connection had not been demonstrated.[4] Wicker examined 20 studies of job attitudes and job behavior, 16 studies of attitudes and behavior toward minority groups, and 11 studies of attitudes and behavior toward miscellaneous objects, such as attendance at union meetings, spending money, voting, and cheating on exams.

S.M. Corey, a professor of educational psychology at the University of Wisconsin, conducted one of the studies reviewed by Wicker.[5] Early on in a course Corey was teaching, he measured students' attitude toward cheating in the classroom "anonymously." During the course, the students self-graded five exams. Without the students realizing it, Professor Corey also graded the exams and related the differences between the students' self-graded scores and their actual scores to the students' attitude toward cheating. The study did find cheating, but found no relation between actual cheating in the classroom and attitude toward cheating in the classroom.

Across the 47 studies, Wicker found that attitudes have little or no relation to behavior.

More recently, some social scientists have sought to resurrect the assumed connection between attitudes and behavior.[6] They noticed that the attitudes investigated in earlier studies were typically general attitudes (for example, feelings about a particular racial group) whereas the behaviors were more specific (for example, renting a room right now to a particular person of that racial group). These social scientists found that the more specific the attitude is to the behavior, the more the attitude and the behavior vary together. An attitude is specific to a behavior if the attitude is about performing that precise behavior, toward a precise target, at a precise time, under precise circumstances. But this is not attitude as we commonly think of attitude.

The attempt to resurrect the assumed connection between attitude and behavior by changing the definition of the attitude to be as delimited as the behavior is an admission of the problem. Attitude, certainly as commonly understood, does not determine behavior.

And attitudes are hard to change. "Intellectual antibodies," to use Naomi Klein's phrase, get in the way.[7] Intellectual antibodies help us preserve our preconceptions. These antibodies are also known as "Confirmatory Bias."[8] Confirmatory Bias is made up of two parts: (1) People tend to seek out information that reinforces their existing attitudes and avoid information that might undermine their existing attitudes, a phenomenon known as "Selective Exposure." Conservatives watch Fox news and liberals watch MSNBC because Fox news reinforces conservatives' attitudes and MSNBC reinforces liberals' attitudes. (2) When information makes it through Selective Exposure, people interpret that information to fit their preconceptions, a phenomenon known as "Selective Perception." Everyone saw the same polling data before the 2012 election. But those who hoped for and expected a Romney victory interpreted ("unskewed") those polls to fit the data to their preconceptions.

Which Is Easier to Change, the Act or the Attitude?

Strange as it seems, the act is easier to change than the attitude.

People who see our behavior believe our actions spring from some deep-seated quality within us.[9] But we interpret our actions quite differently. We see our actions as springing from circumstance. So if circumstances change, we can change what we do and keep our attitude intact.

How people act is a result of both attitude and circumstances. Circumstances have a much greater impact on behavior than we realize. Whereas attitudes resist change, circumstances are often malleable. Change the circumstances and you will change how people act.

Consider all the things you can do to change the circumstances in the home, in the workplace, in the school, or in the store to make the option you recommend more likely.

A persuader can rearrange a circumstance like price, or distribution, or location in store, and change what we buy, but avoid our attitude. A buy-one-get-one-free offer on Cheerios may get us to buy even though we still prefer Corn Flakes. By changing the circumstances, the persuader has avoided our "Intellectual Antibodies."

I may prefer shopping at Wal-Mart to shopping at Kmart. Build a Kmart nearby and there is a good chance I'll shop at Kmart more often even if you don't change my attitude. The circumstances have changed my behavior, but my attitude remains intact.

Changing the circumstances can be easier than buy-one-get-one-free or building a store. You may generally prefer a cookie to a pear. However, when you are hungry, if a pear is at hand and cookies are not, there is a much better chance you will choose the pear. Your behavior may change even though your preference for cookies doesn't.

Many of our actions take place without involving our conscious attitudes. The lizard inside, our automatic, nonconscious mental system, guides a lot of what we do. We often act without careful consideration of pros and cons or how well the action fits our attitude.

William James, the renowned American philosopher and psychologist, said back in 1899, that 99 percent of our activity is purely automatic.[10] Recent psychological research confirms his suggestion. Much of our behavior results from cues in the environment, rather than conscious reflection and deliberation.[11]

If the rack at the checkout counter contains a basket of apples, I might buy an apple rather than a candy bar to snack on during the trip home. My choice would change, but not my attitude toward either apples or candy bars.

When persuading, don't begin by asking, "How can I get people to change their minds?" Ask instead, "How can I get them to act differently?" Getting people to act differently might or might not involve changing their minds.

Thaler and Sunstein's best-selling book, *Nudge*, provides example after example of how an organization or a governmental body can change the circumstances in which people make decisions and, as a result, help those people make better decisions.[12] Better decisions don't require a change of attitude, but they may result in a change of attitude.

Does Attitude Cause Behavior or the Reverse?

Another reason it is useful to target the act rather than the attitude is that what's cause and what's effect are often the opposite of what we expect. A change in behavior is more likely to cause a change in attitude rather than the reverse.

People believe that attitude is cause and behavior is effect. Historically, most social scientists believed that as well. But evidence of the influence of attitude on behavior is inconsistent. Evidence of the influence of behavior on attitude, on the other hand, is pretty strong. If we change the way a person acts, we are likely to change the way that person feels. This turns things upside down. Rather than attitude change being the most promising path to behavior change, it seems that the most promising path may run in the opposite direction.

Evidence of the impact of our actions on our attitudes initially comes from two areas of social psychology known as cognitive dissonance research and self-perception theory.

Cognitive dissonance research found that if you act in a way that is inconsistent with your attitude, you will generally adjust your attitude to fit with your action, that is, you will shift your attitude to justify or rationalize your behavior.[13]

Social psychologists are fond of seeing what happens when people act in ways that are inconsistent with their attitude. To get people to act that way, they conducted a variety of creative experiments. They have asked study participants to tell others that a clearly boring task is actually interesting and engaging.[14] They have asked study participants to write essays arguing in favor of positions that contradict the participants' own attitudes.[15] They have asked participants to eat grasshoppers when the participants would rather not.[16] In each case, social psychologists found that when participants acted in a way that was inconsistent with their attitude, their attitude changed in the direction of their behavior. Their attitude shifted to justify or rationalize their behavior.

Even if people are somewhat indifferent about two items, being forced to choose one option over the other results in a change of attitude. Jack Brehm[17] offered people a choice of two attractive items to take home as a gift. After people chose either one of the items, they felt more positively toward the item they chose and more negatively toward the item they rejected than they did before choosing. After they chose, people adjusted their attitude to rationalize their behavior.

According to the theory of cognitive consistency, inconsistency between action and attitude is uncomfortable and adjusting the attitude reduces the discomfort.

Self-perception theory is a reinterpretation of cognitive dissonance research. According to self-perception theory, we don't really know ourselves. To use Wilson's phrase, we are strangers to ourselves. We infer our own attitudes from how we behave.[18] We figure out who we are by observing what we do.

So, according to self-perception theory, attitude change doesn't necessarily result from the discomfort we feel when our actions are inconsistent with our attitude. Rather, when our actions are inconsistent with our former attitude, we reinterpret our attitude, we reinterpret who we are. We even infer from our behavior attitudes that weren't there before.

I might be careful about what I eat because of pressure from my spouse. But I am likely to come to see myself as someone who is concerned about what I eat and my perception of the influence of the pressure from my spouse on my behavior will recede.

What we do, regardless of the cause, changes our self-definition.

Religion, one of the most powerful forces in society, seems to be dependent on self-perception. Few people objectively examine all religions and choose for themselves the one that is the most compelling. Almost all of us are the same religion as our parents. And our parents' religion was the same as their parents' before them.

If the parents are Catholic, the children go to mass. If the parents are Jewish, the children go to synagogue. If the parents are Muslim, the children go to the mosque. And so on. When asked what their religion is, children look at how they have been behaving and conclude they are that religion. Religious action has a dramatic impact on religious attitude. Even though religious attitude is often based on childhood religious behavior, that religious attitude can still be strong enough to change lives or take lives.

Self-perception theory is sometimes applied in psychotherapy in which clients are encouraged to change their behavior in expectation that this behavior change will result in attitude change. Self-perception theory has even been used to reduce teen pregnancy. When teens do volunteer work in their community, they feel more a part of the fabric of the community and are less likely to take risks in their behavior.[19] When teens do volunteer work in their community, they reinterpret who they are and this, in turn, affects how they behave.

Of course, this works for much more than teen pregnancy. If we encourage our teens to do volunteer work in our community, our teens will observe their own behavior and redefine who they are; they will redefine their commitment to the community. It won't matter that we put pressure on them to volunteer. Our teens will define themselves by what they do no matter why they do it.

After many years of decline, uniforms are again springing up in both private and public schools, even in some of the roughest areas. The hope is that by changing the way children dress, the community can change the way children see themselves. Children observe what they are wearing and redefine who they are and how they behave. It is still early, but it seems to be working.[20]

It is difficult to change parental attitudes toward childhood vaccinations. It will probably be easier to change the act. If up-to-date vaccinations are required for school attendance and philosophical and religious exemptions are difficult to obtain, parents will comply. Not only will they comply, they will feel a lot more positively about vaccinations. People's attitude will reflect their behavior.

Changing the circumstances changes the behavior and changing the behavior, in turn, changes the attitude.

Cognitive dissonance research began in the 1950s and self-perception theory dates from the 1960s, but we have only recently begun to understand the body-to-mind connection that underlies the phenomenon.

The lizard uses the body to help think and the actions of the body feedback to the lizard. In research published in 2010, Dana Carney, Amy Cuddy, and Andy Yap simply had people strike two poses, each for one minute.[21] Half the participants positioned themselves in "high-power" poses with expansive limbs and the other half of the participants positioned themselves in "low-power" poses with contracted limbs as in a self-hug. Even though these poses were only held for one minute, the experimenters found that the poses caused "physiological, psychological, and behavioral changes." In particular, they found "elevation of the dominance hormone testosterone, reduction of the stress hormone cortisol, and increases in behaviorally demonstrated risk tolerance and feelings of power." By placing their bodies in a powerful pose, people become more powerful.

In discussing this feedback body to mind, Wilson reminds us of Kurt Vonnegut's advice: "We are what we pretend to be, so we must be careful about what we pretend to be."[22]

Parents sometimes think it's cute to select hairstyles or clothes for their young children that are worn by society's rebels. Mohawks or motorcycle jackets or whatever that, in an older person, would be indicative of a rejection of societal norms can be amusing when worn by a small child who is totally dependent on adults. However, if the child comes to define himself as someone who rejects society's norms, the parents may be in for some challenges. The child will figure out who he is by observing what he does. Why he does it is immaterial. To paraphrase Vonnegut, children may become what we pretend they are, so we should be careful about what we pretend they are.

For the most part, the attitude change that results from behavior change occurs without us being aware of it. In fact, our current actions can cause us to forget or misremember what our original beliefs or attitudes were.[23] Once we act, our attitude toward that action becomes more positive than it was before we acted. And, once we act, we remember our attitude toward that action as more positive than it actually was.

The fact that behavior change often leads to attitude change is the reason why the "gaining commitment" and "foot-in-the-door" approaches are included in lists of surprisingly effective persuasive techniques.

Gaining commitment refers to the technique of getting people to say they would do something because saying they would do something improves the chances they will actually do it.[24]

Jim Sherman, Chancellor's professor of Psychological and Brain Sciences at Indiana University, illustrated the impact of saying we would do something.[25] Sherman called people in Indiana and asked them what they would say *if* they were asked to spend three hours collecting money for the American Cancer Society. Many people said they would volunteer. Days later, when someone apparently from the American Cancer Society did call and ask people to volunteer, three out of 10 of those who had been asked for a commitment agreed and almost all of those who predicted they themselves would volunteer did volunteer. The proportion agreeing to volunteer was seven times higher among those who were called days earlier to predict their behavior than among those who were not asked to predict their behavior.

Whether you are trying to persuade a boss, a friend, or a family member, aim for commitment. Commitment will be much easier to get than actual behavior change, and once you have commitment, behavior change will come more readily.

The foot-in-the-door technique is related. The technique increases the chances of getting people to take a major action by getting them to first take a smaller action in the same direction. Persuading people to take a small action is more feasible and, once they take the small action, their attitude begins to change, making the major persuasion possible. Asking someone to take a small action, like putting a three-inch square sign saying "Be a Safe Driver" in their window can increase compliance threefold with a later request, made by a different person, to put a very large sign on the lawn saying "Drive Carefully."[26]

If you are trying to organize your neighbors to confront city hall about needed improvements, start small. Get your foot in the door. Start with a block party, then a petition, and you may be able to work your way up to a march on the mayor's office.

Action adjusts perception, leaving the situation looking different to the actor.

When you change the act, there is a good chance you will affect the attitude. When you change the attitude, there is a good chance you will not affect the act.

Tools to Change the Act

Possibly the most important reason to aim at the act rather than the attitude is that aiming at the act allows you, the persuader, to choose from a much wider array of persuasive tools. When you take stock of what you can do to accomplish your goal, you can, of course, use all the techniques that might change attitude if that is your chosen path to behavior change. But you also can use a whole host of other techniques for changing behavior that don't run afoul of "Intellectual Antibodies."

With consumer products, you can change the act by changing the price, changing the distribution, changing the packaging, getting someone else in the household to ask for the product, enhancing the product's presence in the grocery store with promotional displays, and so on.

When going door-to-door, canvassing for a political candidate in Iowa, I had no success changing anyone's attitude toward the candidates. People's attitudes were firmly in favor, firmly against, or firmly undecided and my visit wasn't about to change that. Though I couldn't change attitudes, I found I could change behavior. Potential voters were eager to know where and when early voting was taking place. I was told which voters were leaning toward my candidate. All I had to do was to contact those voters and give them the early voting information and I influenced behavior without changing attitude.

When helping a political candidate, you can change the vote by getting those already leaning toward your candidate to vote early, locking up their vote. You can make sure that those leaning toward your candidate, but who haven't voted early definitely get to the polling station on Election Day. In neither case have you changed attitudes toward your candidate, but you have influenced voting behavior.

When working to further a pro-choice or pro-life agenda, you can work to defeat an incumbent at the polls rather than working to change the incumbent's attitude. If you are successful, other office holders may change their behavior without changing their attitude because they fear a similar fate.

As parents we don't have to change our children's attitude toward empty calorie foods. If we can fill the kids up with fresh fruit and oatmeal, they'll eat less Fruit Loops even if their attitude toward Fruit Loops is unchanged.

When we aim at the act, we don't need to aim at the ultimate act.

Microsoft has decided to aim at the act, but not the ultimate act. Ultimately, Microsoft wants people to buy Microsoft products. But its approach doesn't aim at changing people's attitude toward Microsoft. Rather, Microsoft has invited everyone who has Windows 7 or 8 to download Windows 10 for free. Microsoft doesn't make money by offering a free download of their new operating system. But everyone who downloads Windows 10 is more likely to purchase other Microsoft products and is less likely to switch to a Mac. Microsoft gets their foot in the door by providing a free download of Windows 10. Once Windows 10 is downloaded, users attitudes toward Microsoft improve a bit and users are more likely buy many other pieces of software that Microsoft offers.

Bisquick is a popular baking mix sold by General Mills. Bisquick marketing also illustrates aiming at the act, but not the ultimate act. Obviously, the brand would like people to purchase Bisquick. However, it seems that most people who might be interested in purchasing Bisquick already have a box of Bisquick on their shelf. When they use up the Bisquick on their shelf, they purchase another box. Until then, they don't.

Using Bisquick is an intermediate act. Purchasing Bisquick is the ultimate act.

Brand management can get more people to purchase Bisquick by getting people to use up the Bisquick they already have. So Bisquick aims at getting people to use up the Bisquick on their shelf. Bisquick encourages people to impress their family with a dish that uses the Bisquick they already have in the pantry. Bisquick doesn't spend time telling people why Bisquick is superior to other options. It simply encourages people to prepare a dish like pancakes, biscuits, Impossible Pie, or one of the many other recipes that empty the Bisquick box.

As it is sometimes useful to aim our persuasive efforts at some intermediate act rather than our ultimate goal, how do we pick an intermediate act?

The Leaky Hose

Any physical action is actually the end point of a series of steps. Take the time to lay out the steps. It's helpful to think of this series of steps as a leaky hose. Many people fail to make it to the end, because they leak out somewhere along the way. The pool of potential people who might behave as we would like shrinks as they take or fail to take a series of action steps toward the ultimate action goal.

Think about all the people who might ultimately behave as you would like. What is the series of action steps that leads to the ultimate behavior you seek? How many people "leak out" at each step? Ask yourself, "Where do you lose potential?"

Think about a major choice such as buying a car. We laid out the steps leading to the purchase of a Volkswagen in the following way:

- Make a short list of cars to consider.

- Gather information on those cars from magazines or television.

- Ask friends, relatives, or owners of the cars on that short list.

- Check out the brands' own Websites.

- Check out Websites that compare brands.

- Visit the dealer.

- Take a test drive.

- Negotiate a price.

- Purchase.

You can expand the list, shorten it, or modify it based on your understanding of the process involved. Once you have your list, you can ask how many potential buyers you lose at each step and how feasible it is to patch that leak.

If you are failing to get on the short list because you are a foreign make and many people want to buy a car made in the United States, you might explain that your cars are actually made in Tennessee. If you have a great Website but not enough people are visiting, you can figure out how to attract more people to your online site. If you're getting people in the showroom but not enough are taking a test drive, you might put in place a program of training for salespeople. A smile, a firm handshake, or a remembered first name could be enough to increase test drives.

As you lay out the leaky hose, you might come up with a plan that has several different elements for what you can do in mass media, in social media, on your Website, and in the dealership to move people through the leaky hose. Those in the business world call this an integrated marketing program.

One can lay out the steps in any number of ways. The value is in breaking down the larger action into a series of smaller choices that each may be more easily influenced.

Sometimes the choice is lightning quick and largely automatic. However, even a decision as simple as the choice made at home of an apple instead of a cookie can be thought of as the end point of a series of action steps. We can lay out those action steps and think about where we might lose someone along the way. We may be able get apples chosen more frequently by simply making apples more visible in our kitchen and cookies less visible. It may be possible to influence some intermediate choice (placing apples on the counter and cookies in the cabinet) in a way that might not have occurred to us if we were focusing only on the ultimate choice (apple or cookie as snack).

Persuading someone to place apples on the counter and cookies in the cabinet will probably be easier than persuading someone to eat an apple rather than a cookie when they are about to make a choice between those two equally available snacks.

When the ultimate action is one we want to encourage, we want to reduce the leaks and keep people moving through the hose. We ask at each step why are people leaking out of the hose? What are those people doing instead of what we would like them to do?

Being clear about the "instead of" helps sharpen our persuasive attempt.

Imagine we want people to purchase Rolled Gold Pretzels. Anyone buying a salty snack is a potential customer. We may look at how many people who buy a salty snack buy pretzels. And we might look at how many people who buy pretzels buy Rolled Gold Pretzels.

We could increase Rolled Gold sales by getting more people to buy pretzels instead of some other salty snack. If more people buy pretzels, Rolled Gold will get its share. To encourage people to buy pretzels instead of some other salty snack, we might emphasize the rewards of eating pretzels rather than eating the typical salty snack.

On the other hand, we could increase Rolled Gold sales by getting more people to buy Rolled Gold instead of other pretzels. Obviously, to do this we would emphasize the rewards of eating Rolled Gold instead of other pretzels.

Which leak are we going to try to fix? Getting people to buy pretzels instead of some other salty snack is a lot different than getting people to buy Rolled Gold instead of other pretzels. Being clear about the "instead of" sharpens our persuasive attempt.

Let's return to the car-buying example. If many people are going to our brand's Website but few take the next step of visiting our dealership, we have to ask what those people are doing instead.

If visitors to our Website go on to visit the showrooms of other brands but not ours, we have to figure out why. We might ask which specific competitors are getting the visits and what reward these potential buyers anticipate from visiting those showrooms. In the light of that information, we might change our Website, emphasizing different benefits to expect from visiting our brand's showroom.

If visitors to our Website postpone buying a car altogether, we might wonder if we are attracting the wrong people to the Website. Maybe we're attracting people who are not serious about buying a new car. In which case, we have to evaluate and modify whatever we are doing to attract people to our Website.

Understanding the "instead of" helps us decide what we can do to reduce the leak.

When the ultimate act is one we wish to discourage, we want to expand the leaks. We ask at each step what the person could be doing instead of staying within the hose and continuing to flow toward the ultimate undesired action.

Perhaps we are trying to persuade an individual to quit smoking—a very tough assignment. We can look at all the steps leading up to lighting a cigarette:

- Purchase a pack of cigarettes at a convenience store, grocery store, or gas station.
- Go somewhere where one can smoke. That is,
  - Leave the workplace.
  - Leave the home.
  - Leave the restaurant or bar.
- Leave some other retail establishment.
- Take out the pack.
- Open the pack.
- Take out the cigarette.
- Light it.

Knowing the actor personally would enable you to do a much better job of laying out the leaky hose.

In this case, we don't want to patch the leak; we want to enlarge the leak.

One might change who is the primary shopper so the smoker is less often at the point of purchase. Or one might attempt to get a smoker to pay at the pump rather than go in the service station and be subject to temptation. Can the act of taking out the cigarette pack be delayed by encouraging the smoker to put their cigarettes in a less-accessible place? Can other things like sticks of gum be put in the cigarette pack along with cigarettes so that when the smoker reaches for a cigarette he is confronted with a choice?

Breaking down the behavior into smaller steps suggests ideas for intervention that would otherwise never occur to us.

Bud Light vs. Lite Beer From Miller

Bud Light became the world's largest selling beer, but it struggled in its early days. The beginning of its success is a good illustration of aiming at an intermediate act rather than the attitude.

Lite Beer from Miller dominated the light beer market when Bud Light was introduced. Bud Light initially gained a small share of the light beer market, but its sales quickly stagnated. Bud Light couldn't seem to get growing against this massive category leader.

Wholesalers for Anheuser-Busch, the company that brewed Bud Light, explained the situation this way. Young men drink the most beer and the preferences of young men are often determined by what they consume in a bar. Lite Beer from Miller had a tremendous advantage in the bar. A young man would often say to the bartender, "Gimme a light." Both the young man and the bartender interpreted this as "Gimme a L-I-T-E," a request both for a type of beer and a brand. Because few people were asking for Bud Light by name, Bud

Light was having trouble holding on to bar taps. As a result, Bud Light was not growing.

Bud Light could have attempted to get the brand growing by changing beer drinkers' attitudes toward Bud Light and toward Lite Beer from Miller. But the brand chose to aim at an intermediate act. Asking for a Bud Light instead of asking for the brand whose name was synonymous with the category would have been a big step, so Bud Light did not choose the ultimate goal as the aiming point. Bud Light aimed at a smaller, more achievable, but still effective step— getting beer drinkers to hesitate for a moment rather than making the automatic "Gimme a light" request. If young men simply hesitated, realizing they had a choice, Bud Light would grow its small share.

If you are old enough, you may remember a series of simple 10-second TV spots in which a beer drinker would say "Gimme a light." Instead of a beer, he would get some other sort of light—a stop light, a train crossing light, a lighthouse light, a flaming arrow, or whatever. The announcer reinforced the visual by saying that "When you just ask for a light, you never know what you'll get."

One might debate the humor of the spots, but not their impact. Bud Light started to grow as soon as the series of "Funny Light" ads began to run. Aiming at the act of hesitation started the brand on a growth trend that continued until the brand became the best-selling beer in the world.

To persuade people to act differently, you don't have to aim at the ultimate action you desire. Whatever people do is the end of a series of action steps. You may find it easier to aim to change a prior step in the series. Lay out the leaky hose—the series of smaller action steps that lead to the ultimate act you would like to encourage or discourage. Figure out precisely where to focus your persuasive attempt to have the biggest impact on the outcome.

Aim at the act, not the attitude. Changing the act is your ultimate goal. Fortunately, the act may be easier to change than the attitude. And changing the act is likely to be a more effective way of changing the attitude rather than the reverse.

The easiest way to get people to act as you would like is to change the circumstances, making that act seem more natural, normal, and inevitable. And as you focus on an act, make that act appealing to the lizard. The lizard pays attention to how readily the act comes to mind. The lizard is concerned with the associations that are called forth by the act. The lizard notices how the people who perform that act behave and infers the qualities of the group the lizard would, in effect, join if it also performed that act. The lizard will be strongly affected by the emotion that the act evokes. Even mild affection can make a big difference. And the lizard is sensitive to the popularity of the act.

In focusing on the act, building its mental availability and associations, and drawing attention to related behaviors, emotions, and the preferences of others, you are redefining the act. You are giving the act meaning. An act with meaning might be thought of as an act with direction. It is an act that is going somewhere.

Recycling may be thought of as dropping an aluminum can in an identified container. Or recycling can be thought of as something bigger, such as a contribution to a cleaner environment or a small step toward a more efficient government.

Redefine the act. Give it meaning. When you attach associations to the act you transform the act from an objective operation into a subjective, symbolic performance. If you do, you not only increase the probability of the act, you begin to change the attitude toward it.

5

DON'T CHANGE DESIRES, FULFILL THEM

A senior group of clergy, interested in modern persuasion techniques, once visited our advertising agency. One clergyman asked, "How do you change what people want?" I thought for a minute and replied, "We don't try to change what people want. It is too difficult and too expensive. Rather than changing what people want, we use what people want to sell products."

I knew I had not put that well when the clergyman looked at me and said, "Son, you are on a long and slippery slope."

Years later I came across a quote that said what I was trying to say much more clearly. The quote comes from Dale Carnegie:[1]

"The only way on earth to influence people is to talk about what they want, and show them how to get it."

Dale Carnegie intuitively understood *How to Win Friends and Influence People*. But science has only recently figured out how and why it works that way.

We naturally think persuasion means changing what people want. But the lizard isn't interested in changing what it wants. Successful persuasion doesn't try. Successful persuasion shows the lizard a more promising way to get what it already wants.

The lizard inside pursues what it desires. Persuasion encourages a particular pathway to that desire.

We work to associate the fulfillment of a desire, a reward, with the pathway or action we suggest. The reward must be something the target already wants. So we examine how the desires of the people we wish to persuade overlap with the possible outcomes of the action we suggest.

In choosing a car, males look for more excitement and females, especially moms, look for more safety. As a result, males are a little less interested in purchasing a Volvo than females. The way to sell more Volvos to males is not to change what males want. It is not to convince males that they want safety instead of excitement. The way to sell more Volvos to males is to show them that driving a Volvo is exciting. For males, Volvo can be a different and better pathway to excitement because it is the one fun-to-drive car that their spouse will be happy with. The way to sell more Volvos to males is to talk about what males want and to show them they can get it by buying a Volvo.

Adolescents want independence, freedom from adult restraint. Staying in school is the opposite. No wonder adolescents want to drop out of school. The way to keep adolescents in school is not to change what adolescents want. The way to keep adolescents in school is to show them a better pathway to what they want. That better pathway is graduation, the easiest way to get the independence and freedom they seek. Anything short of graduation is likely to keep them under the thumb of adults for a long time.

Speaking of adolescents, we had a couple of adolescent boys in a large bedroom heated by electric baseboard heat and cooled by a window air conditioner. The electric meter spun a lot faster than we liked because we had trouble getting the boys to live with a little lower temperature in the winter and a little higher temperature in the summer. We talked to them about the environmental effects of energy and the cost of energy, but our attempt to change their desires seemed to go in one ear and out the other.

We decided instead to show them how to get something they wanted by doing what we wanted. The bill from the electric company gave us both kilowatt-hours used per month and the cost of a kilowatt-hour. I found I could easily estimate what our electric bill would be if our usage was the same as the previous year's. We told the boys that they could have the money we saved by reducing our electricity use. Because they never had much of an allowance, this was a big deal. They could get what they wanted, money, by doing what we wanted, reducing electricity use. Rather than changing their desire to blast the heat in the winter and the cool air in the summer, we showed them how to fulfill their desire for money by reducing electricity consumption. It radically changed their behavior. From then on, the room was chilly in the winter and warm in the summer and the boys were thrilled.

Dr. Dena Gromet is a postdoctoral research fellow with the Risk Management and Decision Processes Center at The Wharton School (University of Pennsylvania). She studies how the features of a situation and the decision-makers' values affect their choices. Gromet and her colleagues recently published a study in the *Proceedings of the National Academy of Sciences* that illustrated the importance of fulfilling desires, not trying to change desires.[2]

In Gromet's study, consumers were offered a choice between more expensive, more efficient compact florescent light bulbs (CFL) and less expensive, less efficient conventional light bulbs. Conservatives and liberals were equally likely to choose the more expensive, more efficient CFLs when the CFLs' packaging had no environmental message.

The addition of a label saying "Protect the environment" made conservatives less likely to choose the same CFLs. The "Protect the environment" label had no effect on the choices of liberals.

The results puzzled the pundits. How could the addition of an environmental message make the CFLs less attractive to conservatives? How could the addition of an environmental message make the CFLs no more attractive to liberals?

Though puzzling, these results fit what N.H. Andersen found out about how people make judgments. Norman H. Andersen was a social psychologist and Distinguished professor emeritus at the University of California, San Diego. He spent his time studying how people combine information to form positive or negative judgments. He is given credit for developing Information Integration Theory. Professor Andersen found that when people combine information to form a judgment, they don't add, they average.

Efficiency seems a good reward for all consumers; say an 8 on a scale from 1 to 10. So all consumers are equally likely to choose CFLs when efficiency is the only reward offered.

Protecting the environment, however, is not a believable reward for conservatives, say a 2 on a scale from 1 to 10. People don't add. They average. The average of 8 and 2 is 5. When the environmental message was added, conservatives should be less likely to choose CFLs and they were. The combined message is less appealing than the efficiency message alone. I suspect that when the environment was given as an additional reason to purchase CFLs, consumers who normally put little faith in an environmental reward also put less faith in the efficiency reward.

Protecting the environment is a believable reward for liberals; say an 8 on a scale from 1 to 10. But people don't add. They average. The average of 8 and 8 is 8. Liberals should be no more likely to choose CFLs when the environmental message was added. That's exactly what happened.

Everybody is motivated by a promise of efficiency. Some people believe and are motivated by a promise of saving the environment. We could attempt to change what conservatives want, hoping to make them choose CFLs to save the environment. But it's probably a waste of time. If we want everyone to use CFLs, efficiency is the way to go.

"The only way on earth to influence people is to talk about what they want, and show them how to get it."

The Gromet, et al. experiment makes a critical point about the importance of fulfilling desires rather than changing desires. That experiment suggests that talking about what people don't want makes whatever you say about what they do want less persuasive.

Whether talking to a friend, a committee, a parent association, or a segment of society, talk about what they want, only about what they want, and show them how to get it.

If you are trying to persuade two targets that have different desires, try to talk to them separately. If you must talk to both groups at once, forget what is most motivating to each individual group and go with the one reward that is most motivating to the total. Trying to talk about two different rewards in the same message will inevitably make you less persuasive.

Someone promoting recycling might be tempted to offer two rewards. If liberals want to save the environment and conservatives want to lower the cost of government, why not offer both rewards and appeal to everyone? Offering both rewards may seem reasonable, but it's a mistake. Adding a second reward will not make your message more motivating. It will make your message less motivating. People don't add; they average. The average of your most powerful reward and any other reward is less than your most powerful reward alone. With recycling, as with CFLs, efficiency will probably be more motivating to the total than saving the environment.

We know we have to talk about something people already want, but people want a lot of things. How do we choose a specific reward out of everything people want?

Think Big

The most common mistake made in choosing which reward to offer is thinking too small. We naturally look for some reward directly following from the act we recommend—a 10-cent savings, more nutrition, a more comfortable bed. But there's no need to limit ourselves in that way. We should think big. We should ask what the lizard wants out of life that might conceivably be related to the act we suggest.

With apologies to Daniel Burnham, a 19th-century architect, for borrowing his idea: Promise no little rewards. They have no magic to stir men's blood.

What do people want out of life that the action you suggest might bring about? Do you want to save 10 cents or be seen as a smarter person? Do you want to get the superior nutrition of a bag of apples over a bag of chips or do you want healthy kids? Do you want cleaner floors or the admiration of friends?

Some desires are common to the human condition. Promise something that most people want. Rewards that are universally desired are more powerful. If a reward appeals to only a narrow segment of the population, it is often a weaker reward even for that narrow segment.

Older people often find modern cell phone technology confusing. In order to appeal to that older segment, you could promise a reward of simplicity and ease of use. But even in selling cell phones to older people, you would probably be better off promising older people that your simple and easy-to-use cell phone gives them that ability to reach out and influence the world that everyone wants from a cell phone. That sense of control is the reward they want. The fact that your particular model of phone is simple and easy to use is why they have a better chance of getting that sense of control from your phone. Simple and easy to use should not be the reward, but should be what people in advertising call a "support point." A support point is something that makes your reward believable. A support point is why your pathway to that fundamental desire is the way to go.

Choose as the reward for doing what you would like something that just about everybody wants. Who doesn't want to be a hero to their kids? Who doesn't want to be appealing to the opposite sex? Who doesn't want to be seen by others as sophisticated, as smart, as healthy, as a good parent? These desires apply to large portions of society, and the opportunity to fulfill these desires is broadly motivating.

Strong motives tend to be universal. Don't be distracted by trivial differences across different groups in your target. *The rewards desired by different groups are not identical, but the similarities in motivation across groups are greater than the differences.*

As we said, marketers are fond of segmentation studies. Segmentation studies divide the population into subgroups that each has a slightly different set of desires motivating their brand choice. Unfortunately, segmentation studies magnify minor differences in desire and mask major commonalities of desire. As a result, marketers are often left studying the trees and missing the forest.

We can look in a variety of places to be reminded of what most people want.

Universal Desires

Abraham Maslow is one of the giants of early psychology. He spent his career at Brooklyn College and then at Brandeis University researching and thinking about mental health and human potential. Back in 1943, Maslow drew upon the psychological tradition of the founders of the field and laid out a classification of human needs that is still in use today.[3]

Maslow said that the first level of need is physiological—water, food, sleep, warmth, exercise, and so on. Once these physiological needs are gratified to some degree, another level of needs arises:

safety needs. Safety needs include peace, a smoothly running society, and economic security. Once safety needs are gratified, love and belongingness needs arise. These include friends, a sweetheart, children, and acceptance in a group. Once love and belongingness needs are gratified, esteem needs arise. Esteem needs include recognition, prestige, and status. When all these other needs are gratified, self-actualization needs arise. Self-actualization entails the desire for challenge, for learning, for creativity, and for innovation.

Maslow himself didn't diagram his classification of human needs, but almost everyone else diagrams Maslow's classification as a pyramid.

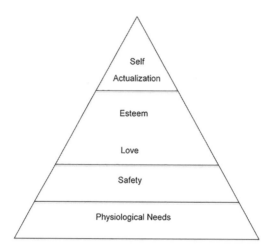

Maslow's Hierarchy of Needs

Another approach to identifying what most people want is to look across all human societies and see what desires seem to be universal. Donald E. Brown, an anthropologist, asks in his book, *Human Universals*, "What do all people, all societies, all cultures, and all languages have in common?"[4] Brown identifies behaviors that are universal. By examining universal behaviors, we can infer universal desires. Brown's list of human universals is long and includes, for example, the following:

- Efforts to increase status.
- Efforts to increase the attractiveness of selves and possessions through decoration.
- Attempts to predict the future.
- Attempts to plan for the future.
- Urge to reciprocate.
- Feelings of empathy.
- Feelings of envy.
- Attempts to communicate more than mere words can communicate.
- Attempts to misinform.
- Efforts to interpret external behavior to grasp internal intention.

From that very incomplete list of universal behaviors, we may infer the following, very incomplete list of universal desires:

- To be seen as superior to others.
- To be seen as attractive and as having attractive possessions.
- To anticipate the future.
- To prepare for the future.
- To repay.
- To feel what others feel.
- To possess what others possess.
- To say more than words alone can convey.
- To occasionally mislead others.
- To understand why someone does what they do.

Examining Maslow's hierarchy of needs and Brown's list of human universals are two useful ways to stimulate our thinking as we look for a powerful reward to offer in persuasion.

Whether the target is few or many, the principle is the same. Think of two circles. One circle represents the desires of the people you are trying to persuade. It contains an almost unlimited number of desires: health, wealth, happy children, feeling sexy, refreshment, popularity, and on and on. A second circle represents all the positive outcomes that might possibly result from taking the action you suggest. Again, this circle contains an almost unlimited number of possible outcomes—feeling like a good parent, better chance at success, cleaner environment, and so on. Then look at the overlap of desires and outcomes; that is, examine the desires that are also possible outcomes of the action you suggest. The reward you should associate with the action lies within that overlap.

The Venn diagram of target desires and action outcomes describes a conceptual, not a mathematical, approach to deciding which reward to offer.

Show people that your recommended option is the best path to what they already desire.

If you want to persuade your teenage son to stay in school, the reward you offer should be both an outcome of staying in school and something he desires. One of his desires may be to spend more time playing video games, but that desire is not in the overlap of target desires and action outcomes. More time to play video games is not an outcome of staying in school. If he stays in school, he can attend the prom. Although that may be an outcome of staying in school, it may not be something your son wants. On the other hand, freedom from adult restraint is both an outcome of staying in school (because staying in school makes it possible to get a good job and get out from under the thumb of parents) and is something your son desires. Freedom from adult restraint is in the intersection of action outcome and target desire. To persuade your teenage son to stay in school, you can talk about what your son wants (freedom from adult restraint) and show him how to get it (staying in school).

Imagine your neighbor has gotten a new dog because he is concerned about crime. Unfortunately, the new dog barks continuously all night. Your neighbor seems unconcerned with the barking because he is a deep sleeper or because he sleeps on the other side of the house. For you, it's a different story. The dog seems to be barking right outside your bedroom window. Let's say your neighbor is not empathetic and doesn't care that his dog is making it hard for you to sleep. You want your neighbor to control his dog's barking. What reward might you associate with that behavior? Look for a reward that is in the intersection of what your neighbor wants and the outcomes of reining in his dog's barking. You might mention how much safer your neighbor would feel if the dog only barked when someone was close to the house, implying that the dog's continuous barking is a lot like the boy who cried wolf. Continuous barking doesn't really increase your neighbor's safety. Increased safety is both something the neighbor wants and an outcome of teaching the dog to bark only when someone is close to the house. You can talk about something your neighbor wants and show him how to get it by doing something you would like him to do.

Intel Inside

Intel illustrates the search for a reward that lies in the overlap of desire and outcome. Intel is a worldwide company that makes computing chips and computing software that can be found in digital products—computers, smartphones, smart TVs, and so on. For many digital products, Intel essentially provides the engine. Intel's target is people who intend to buy digital products. Their goal is to have buyers prefer a digital product with "Intel Inside."

We began by identifying "Digital Dreamers" in several countries around the world with a study that interviewed about 600 people in each county. Digital Dreamers is the label we gave to the roughly 30 percent of the population of each country that intend to buy about three quarters of all digital products. For example, in China, 30 percent of the population intends to purchase three or more digital products accounting for 75 percent of all intended purchases. In the UK, 28 percent of the population intends to purchase four or more digital products accounting for 69 percent of all intended purchases.

We then looked at the desires that seemed to explain why some people become Digital Dreamers.

Some rewards had already been suggested for Intel, such as "human connection" and "peace of mind." But Digital Dreamers feel no more need for human connection and no more need for peace of mind than others in their country. A need for connection or for peace of mind likely did not lead them to become Digital Dreamers.

However, Digital Dreamers do differ from others in consistent ways. Across countries, Digital Dreamers are more likely than others to like the "feeling of speed" and to like sports cars. They are less content than others to stay in the same town for the rest of their lives. They are more optimistic. And they are more likely than others to want to feel like a leader. These differences between Digital Dreamers and others hold among men as well as among women, among younger as well as older consumers, among people who have a managerial or executive job as well as people who don't. Digital Dreamers want something different out of life and that something isn't explained by their gender, age, or job.

We summarized this by saying that people who intend to buy more digital products seek a feeling of exhilaration in their life. Intel, as the engine in digital products, can promise a sense of "exhilaration." That's how a Digital Dreamer feels when using, for example, a hot, new smart phone. If Intel can associate a feeling of exhilaration with the Intel brand, Intel can create demand for products bearing its logo.

The feeling of exhilaration lies in the overlap of the desires of the target and the possible outcomes of purchasing a product with Intel Inside.

If you are selling an electronic device, promise how it will feel to use that device rather than the superior ability to perform some task.

Spend some time thinking about all the desirable outcomes that can occur when someone takes your recommended option. The number of possible rewards will surprise you. Coming up with a set of rewards that might follow from someone acting as you'd like is an exercise in broad thinking and creativity. It sometimes helps to use a grid to stimulate thinking about the rewards that might result from taking your suggested action. A training manual used in our agency contained a grid like the one that follows. It is just one potential device to stimulate thinking and certainly doesn't result in an exhaustive list of possible rewards. The grid asks you to think about functional, sensory, emotional, and expressive rewards that occur when people are about to take the recommended action, while people are taking the recommended action, or after people take the recommended action.

Table 4.1

Possible positive outcomes	Functional	Sensory	Emotional	Expressive
Before the action				
During the action				
Following the action				

Imagine that on behalf of the National Dairy Board we want to encourage people to consume more cheese. Let's say the action we suggest is adding cheese to a dish during meal preparation. What are the positive rewards that might result from this act? Here are some outcomes that might match what people desire.

TABLE 4.2

Possible positive outcomes	Functional	Sensory	Emotional	Expressive
Before the action	Low-cost nutrition	Not applicable	Get a bargain	Feel like a smart shopper
During the action	Easy meal preparation	Smooth and creamy dish	Be creative in the kitchen	Family will praise your cooking
Following the action	Strong bones	Feel healthy	Know your family is getting good nutrition	People will think you are a good mom

In persuasion, we build the "availability" of both the action we encourage and the reward we promise and we enhance the "association" between them. We want both the action and the reward to spring to mind quickly and we want them to be so closely linked that one cannot think of the action without also thinking of the reward. The reward is what people desire. The action is a pathway to that desire. Associating the action with the right reward motivates choice.

The beer wars drove a search for rewards that motivate choice.

When engaged in the beer wars, we looked at physical rewards like real beer taste, quenching thirst, smoothness, and many others. We also looked at emotional or image rewards like feeling or being seen as rugged, intelligent, tough, a leader, and on and on.

When we examined what actually motivated brand choice, we found that all beer drinkers were looking for a brand that fulfilled the same basic set of desires. This is typical. Most users of a category of products are motivated by a similar set of desires. That's why they are category users. Though the desires they seek to fulfill are the same, people chose different brands because they disagree which brands are best able to fulfill those desires.

We found the rewards that motivated young men's beer brand choice were quite similar to the rewards that motivated older men's beer brand choice. Both groups were seeking to fulfill the same basic set of desires.

Similarities in motivation across groups are greater than differences.

Physical rewards of beer brand choice, like taste and refreshment, naturally follow from consumption. Emotional or social rewards of beer brand choice, like feeling or being seen as rugged, fun, or sophisticated, are based on perceptions of the people who drink those brands. By choosing a particular brand, you become one of those people.

We found that social perceptions of a brand and its users could predict brand choice twice as accurately as perceptions of the physical qualities of a brand of beer. We concluded that emotional and social rewards are much more motivating of brand choice than physical rewards. Focusing exclusively on physical rewards of beer drinking would have been thinking small and would have ignored the more important basis of brand choice.

Unless the target is physically deprived—hungry, thirsty, sleepy, and so on—emotional rewards are often more motivating than physical rewards.

Although both younger men and older men found emotional, social rewards more motivating than physical rewards, the difference was even greater for younger men. We found this same pattern when examining other categories such as cell phones, auto repair, computers, and phone service providers.

A couple of more factors should be considered when choosing which reward to associate with an action out of all the rewards that could be associated:

1. How soon would the reward occur?

2. How sure can we be of the reward?

The lizard seeks immediate and certain rewards.

Immediate

If offered a choice between $100 and $110, everyone chooses $110. When time is included, things change. If offered a choice between $100 now and $110 in a month, many people would choose the $100 now. Economists refer to the power of the immediate over the de-layed as "present-biased preference."[5] When choosing, people weigh immediate outcomes more heavily than distant outcomes, a lot more heavily.[6]

Delay diminishes any reward. Promise something people can have now or can feel now.

If trying to talk someone into using CFLs (compact florescent light bulbs) instead of incandescent light bulbs, don't bother talking about annual savings. Explain that CFLs can start saving the user three quarters of the cost of the electricity immediately. So if an in-candescent bulb cost 40 cents to run for a day, an equivalent CFL would cost only about 10 cents a day to run.

Unfortunately, actions that are better for us often have delayed benefits, but immediate costs. Choosing an apple over a piece of choc-olate cake, saving today for retirement, stopping smoking to lessen the risk of cancer all have delayed benefits, but immediate costs.

Certain

Which would you choose?

Option 1: a sure $30

or

Option 2: an 80-percent chance of $45 and
a 20-percent chance of nothing

Almost four out of five people choose the sure \$30.[7] However, the rules of rationality and math say everyone should choose Option 2 because the "expected value" of Option 2 is \$36. The "expected value" of Option 2 is the average result of Option 2 if you repeated it 1,000 times.[8]

A certain reward is far more motivating than an uncertain reward even if the uncertain reward has a very high probability.[9]

The motivating power of a certain reward relative to a highly likely but uncertain reward is far greater than probability says it should be. Certainty has greater psychological value than mathematical value.

Immediacy and certainty are no doubt related in people's minds. Even if we are told that the delayed reward is just as certain as the immediate reward, I suspect people don't completely believe it. \$100 today seems certain. \$110 in a week is not just delayed, there's a possibility that something will intervene and the \$110 won't happen.

Smoking and cancer illustrate simultaneous delay and uncertainty. Whereas the nicotine hit is both immediate and certain, avoiding cancer is both delayed and uncertain.

Just as actions that are good for us tend to have delayed benefits and immediate costs, they also tend to have uncertain benefits and certain costs. Actions that are enticing but bad for us typically have the opposite. No wonder it is so hard to choose the "good for us" path.

The Ad Council in 2009 created a series of ads designed to get us to save money by changing our behavior in specific ways. The Ad Council wanted us to (1) make coffee at home instead of buying expensive coffee shop coffee, (2) brown bag it to work rather than buying our lunch, (3) cook dinner for ourselves rather than ordering take-out food, and (4) drink tap water rather than buying bottled water. The reward offered in each case was far in the future. The reward offered was the amount of money you would save during one year or even 10 years. The ads were doomed because the lizard doesn't want to wait a year or 10 years for a reward. If the lizard is going to initiate some action now, it wants to be assured of a reward now.

The lizard, our automatic, nonconscious mental system, has a strong preference for immediate and certain rewards. Fortunately, it is often possible to translate delayed and uncertain rewards into immediate and certain rewards by focusing on feelings. We'll talk about how this happens in Chapter 7.

Unique or Motivating: an Easy Choice

Marketers often waste a lot of time looking for a reward that no one else is promising. This isn't necessary.

The reward we promise for taking the action we recommend doesn't have to be unique.

To be successful, we just need to associate that reward more closely with the recommended action than with any alternative action.

Miller High Life vs. Budweiser

Associational battles for desirable rewards are common in marketing. Miller High Life began the marvelous "Miller Time" campaign in the 1970s. Each commercial showed rugged men getting off of work and heading for the bar. The commercials sang, "When it's time to relax, one beer stands clear, Miller beer." Miller High Life happened to be one of the few beers in a clear bottle. The "Miller Time" phrase is still understood today. The action recommended was asking for a Miller High Life. The reward was feeling the manly satisfaction of a job well done. It didn't matter if you had a white-collar job, or if you had just finished mowing the lawn, or hadn't really done anything lately. Surely you did something worthwhile in the past and could feel the satisfaction of a job well done. The campaign gave the brand a growth spurt for years.

Budweiser felt threatened. But rather than attempt to build an association between Budweiser and a different reward, Budweiser decided to build an even stronger association with the same reward. Budweiser decided to take the Miller High Life reward and claim it for its own. Budweiser responded with a salute to the workingman, "For all you do, this Bud's for you." Heavy spending behind consistent, highly visible, well executed commercials succeeded in building even stronger association between Budweiser and the manly satisfaction of a job well done. Miller High Life abandoned the "Miller Time" campaign and fell into decline.[10]

Energizer vs. Duracell

The household battery category has for many years been a contest between Duracell and Energizer. Early on, Duracell seized "long lasting" as their reward and hammered this association home. We won the assignment to do advertising for Energizer and immediately set out to find some other reward we could associate with Energizer. Because Duracell had built such a close association between the Duracell brand and the reward of long lasting, we felt we needed to look elsewhere.

We spent a long time looking. One promising idea was sound quality—with Energizer your music will sound better. That idea was compelling. People would buy Energizer rather than Duracell if Energizer made their music sound better. Unfortunately, we couldn't say it because it wasn't true. No matter how hard we tried, we could not relate power source to sound quality.

Finally, we gave up looking for an alternative. Long lasting is the one thing that is the basis of battery choice.

We could say that current Energizer batteries last a lot longer than earlier versions of Energizer batteries. Of course, Duracell could say the same: that current Duracell batteries last a lot longer than earlier versions of Duracell batteries. But neither Energizer nor Duracell could say they last longer than the other brand. On long lasting, the two brands were equal.

Though Energizer was equal to Duracell on long lasting in reality, Duracell was associated in consumer minds with long lasting and we, Energizer, were not. Duracell batteries were selling better than Energizer batteries.

We had no alternative but to tackle Duracell head-on and try to build an even stronger association with long lasting. We came up with the irrepressible Energizer Bunny and even made the first Energizer Bunny ad, but we lost the account anyway. For us, the Energizer Bunny was one idea among many for building the association between Energizer and long lasting. We didn't see the potential power of the Bunny.

During the meeting with the Energizer marketing director, we showed our ideas for enhancing the association of Energizer with long lasting. Most of the ideas did not involve the Bunny. The marketing director asked if we had any more ideas for how to use the Bunny. We did not. We knew we were in trouble. He had obviously seen something from another agency that he liked.

That other agency, TBWA, saw more clearly the magic in the Energizer Bunny. They suggested making the Energizer Bunny the centerpiece of every ad. They created pretend ads for other products that the Energizer Bunny, beating his drum and clashing his cymbal, would interrupt and march through because the Energizer Bunny just keeps going and going. TBWA transformed the Energizer Bunny into a universal symbol for never tiring and successfully associated Energizer batteries with long lasting.

Regardless of the ups and downs in the agency business, sometimes the search for a different reward is a waste of time. Occasionally, only one reward matters.

The reward we promise doesn't have to have been never promised before, or not promised by alternative actions. We just need to associate that reward more closely with our recommended action than it is associated with any alternative action.

If the reward we associate with the action we recommend is both motivating and unique, that's great. But if we have to choose, we are much better off with a motivating reward than a unique reward. Remember: Many unique rewards are not promised by others because they are not motivating.

Persuasion is about fulfilling desires, not changing desires. To be successful in persuasion, we have to talk about what the target wants. When we stop trying to change what people want and instead try to show people how to get what they want, our message becomes dramatically different. Our persuasive attempts become less strident, preachy, and moralistic, and more focused on the desires of the target. Only then will the target listen.

6

NEVER ASK, UNEARTH

Bill Bernbach was a gifted, intuitive persuader and the father of the creative revolution in advertising. He said, "At the heart of an effective creative philosophy is the belief that nothing is so powerful as an insight into human nature, what compulsions drive a man, what instincts dominate his action...."[1]

Whether we are trying to get the public to change, trying to get voters to change, trying to get shoppers to change, or trying to get a family member to change, we need an insight into the compulsions and instincts that drive their current behavior.

But what is an insight?

Though we are not sure what an insight is, we sense its absence. In any organization, the surest way to undermine a proposed persuasion attempt is to complain that "It contains no insight." The criticism is both deadly and irrefutable. Explanation can't make an insight insightful any more than explanation can make a joke funny.

Jokes and insights, it turns out, have a lot in common. We can learn something from the comparison. Both jokes and insights are defined by their effect. A joke makes us laugh. Otherwise, it's not a joke. An insight gives us the pleasure of a surprising truth. Otherwise, it's not an insight.

A formula for jokes or insights doesn't exist, but every good joke and every good insight has three qualities: They are unexpected, provocative, and true.

Unexpected

We've long known that jokes involve a setup and a surprise. A traditional definition of a joke and one that the noted humorist Sigmund Freud used is "bewilderment succeeded by illumination."

A man gets a call from his doctor. The doctor says, "Thank god I've reached you. I have bad news and worse news."

"Oh dear, what's the bad news?" asks the patient.

The doctor replies, "The results of your tests came back saying you have only 24 hours to live."

"That's terrible," says the patient. "How can the news possibly be worse?"

The doctor replies, "I've been trying to reach you since yesterday."

Insights require the same setup and surprise, the same sort of "bewilderment succeeded by illumination." I suspect that more jokes and insights fail from a weak setup than from a week punch line. Insufficient bewilderment diminishes illumination.

Provocative

Both a joke and an insight juxtapose the incongruous to make us stop and think.

An old man was sitting on a park bench staring at a teenage boy who had spiked yellow, red, green, and orange hair.

The young man says, "What's the matter, old man...didn't you do anything wild in your day?"

"Well...," says the old man, "made love to a parrot once. Thought you might be my son."

True

The element of truth gives a joke its edge. Truth seen from a new angle gives an insight its power.

A horse walks into a bar. The bartender asks: "So, why the long face?"

Persuasion requires an insight into the target, a fresh perspective that is unexpected, provocative, and true.

Where can we find that?

Language Camouflage

Let's take a look at the rest of that Bill Bernbach quote. "At the heart of an effective creative philosophy is the belief that nothing is so powerful as an insight into human nature, what compulsions drive a man, what instincts dominate his action **even though his language so often camouflages what really motivates him.**"

A person's language hides his motivation. The camouflage isn't meant to be deceptive. It's not even voluntary. People just don't know what motivates them.

To persuade, we need to know why people do what they do and what might cause them to change.

To find out, never ask.

Motivations don't reveal themselves to frontal assault. People couldn't tell us their motivations even if they wanted to.

Asking people why they do what they do, or how they choose, or what's most important in their decision is a lousy way to find out. If we ask, we will get an answer, but we will likely get the wrong answer. People don't lie. They just don't know "Why?" But they think they do.

Because our decisions are made by or heavily influenced by the lizard inside, our automatic, nonconscious mental system, we simply don't have access to "Why?" We are not conscious of "Why?" We cannot say how motives and perceptions that are invisible to us influence our behavior.[2]

Amazingly, even though we don't know "Why?" we are sure we do know. If asked "Why?" we instantly answer. We are extremely good at making up answers to why we behave the way we do. We come up with the answers quickly and effortlessly and we believe them to be true.

We have learned that people can't tell us why they do what they do from studies of brain-damaged people, studies of people under hypnosis, and studies of normal people.

The story of a patient called P.S. is one of the most fascinating.[3] P.S. suffered from severe epilepsy. Because epileptic seizures can spread from one hemisphere of the brain to the other, doctors severed the right hemisphere of his brain from the left, a dramatic operation but one that improved his condition.

In a normal brain, there is a lot of cross-communication between the two halves. But the two halves of P.S.'s brain could not communicate. The surgery that severed the connection between the two halves of his brain diminished the effects of his epilepsy, but there were other consequences as well. For example, the left half of P.S.'s brain lost its link with language whereas the right side remained fluent.

These unfortunate circumstances did permit psychologists to do some interesting experiments.

Our right brain receives the information from light passing through our left eye. Our left brain receives the information from light passing through our right eye.

Psychologists rigged a system in which one picture could be shown to P.S.'s right brain (that is, shown to his left eye) and simultaneously a different picture could be shown to P.S.'s left brain (that is, shown to his right eye). The image shown to the right brain was a chicken claw. The image shown to the left brain was a snow scene. In a normal person this would be uncomfortable because the two halves of the brain would communicate and try to reconcile the different images. But with P.S., the two halves were not communicating.

Psychologists also gave P.S. a set of cards showing other objects. They asked him to pick the card that matched the picture he saw. His right hand, controlled by his left brain, which saw the snow scene, pointed at a shovel. His left hand, controlled by his right brain, which saw the chicken claw, pointed at a chicken. All of this made complete sense. However, when asked why he picked those two things, P.S. answered without hesitation, "Oh, that's easy. The chicken claw goes with the chicken and you need a shovel to clean out the chicken shed." His right brain, where his language capability resided, had only seen the chicken claw and did not see the snow scene. It did not know why one of his hands pointed at a shovel, but it immediately made up a rational explanation for his behavior.

People often don't know why they do what they do. But, if asked, they will come up with an answer and believe it to be true. Unfortunately, the answer they come up with may have no connection to reality.

In a similar way, people do things under hypnotic suggestion and don't know why. But these people quickly make up a rational explanation for their behavior and they believe the explanation they offer.

According to David Eagleman, "We have ways of retrospectively telling stories about our actions as though the actions were always our idea." And, "We are constantly fabricating and telling stories about the alien processes running under the hood."[4]

Richard Nisbett is professor of social psychology and co-director of the Culture and Cognition program at the University of Michigan at Ann Arbor. Nisbett and Timothy Wilson conducted a simple experiment in which normal people described why they made an everyday choice.[5] The two scientists set up a table in the front of a Meijer's Thrifty Acres just outside Ann Arbor, Michigan. A sign was on the table saying "Consumer Evaluation Survey—Which Is the Best Quality?" On the same table were four pairs of nylon panty hose arranged from left to right and labeled A, B, C, and D. Once people chose the one pair they felt was the best quality, researchers asked them why they had chosen that pair. In response, "People typically pointed to an attribute of their preferred pair, such as its superior knit, sheerness, or elasticity. No one spontaneously mentioned that the position of the panty hose had anything to do with their preference." When asked, all respondents but one denied that position had anything to do with their choice.

In fact, all four pairs of panty hose were identical. Position was the only difference. As in previous research, people preferred the option on the right with 12 percent picking pair A, 17 percent picking pair B, 31 percent picking pair C, and 40 percent picking pair D. People chose one pair of panty hose out of four either on the basis of position or randomly. There was no factual basis to do so. They then immediately made up a rational reason for their choice, a reason they themselves believed.

Nisbett and Wilson found that people can only tell us what they think they know about how they think, but not how they actually think.

Market researchers are quite familiar with this phenomenon. Researchers distinguish between "reported importance" and "revealed importance." Reported importance is what people say is important in their choice. Revealed importance is what is shown by analysis to be actually related to choice. What's revealed to be important is often surprising.

Another experiment by Nisbett and Wilson concerns our ability to recognize why we are attracted to another person. If asked, we could surely say why we did or did not find the other person alluring. But do we really know why?

In a park in British Columbia, an attractive female assistant of Nisbett and Wilson approached young men and asked if they would be willing to fill out a questionnaire. The cover story was that the woman was involved in a class project on the impact of scenic attractions on creativity. After the young men filled out the questionnaire, the woman thanked them and offered to explain the study when she had more time. She tore off a corner of the questionnaire, wrote her phone number, and told each young man to call her if they wanted to talk to her about the details of the study. What researchers really wanted to know was how many men were sufficiently attracted to the interviewer to call her and ask her for a date.

The female assistant approached half of the men while they were on a narrow footbridge that swayed in the breeze over a deep gorge. She approached the rest of the men when they were seated on a bench after they had crossed the bridge. Which men were more attracted to the interviewer? Which men would be more likely to call her and ask her for a date? Would there be any difference? After all, it was the same interviewer for all participants.

Of the men approached on the bridge, 65 percent called the woman and asked for a date. Of the men approached while seated on the bench, 30 percent called her and asked for a date.

The experimenters theorized that the men approached on the bridge received the interviewer's phone number when "their heart was beating rapidly, they were a bit short of breath, and they were perspiring."[6] The experimenters predicted that these men would misattribute some of their arousal to feelings of attraction to the woman. They were right.

If asked why they called to ask for a date, none of the men would have said "because my heart was beating rapidly when she gave me her number."

The behavior of our body feeds back to our brain, but our consciousness is not in the loop. Our conscious mind does not know why we do what we do.

Okay, so people don't know why they do what they do. What harm can there be in asking them?

Asking people "Why?" will send us in the wrong direction because bad information is worse than no information, a lot worse. We can't seem to resist believing bad information even though we know it's worthless. Kahneman's research tells us that our automatic, non-conscious mental system will treat even bad information as if it were true.[7] That is the way the system works and it works that way even among people who should know better. Even doctors, reporters, and scientists find it hard to resist information they know is worthless.

Despite the fact that "Why?" is a poor question to put to a respondent, "Why?" is still a common question in market research and political research. The boss wants to know the answer and those who are supposed to get answers can't think of any other way to get them.

The answers pollsters get to questions about the qualities voters look for in a candidate are worse than useless. The answers are more likely to mislead than to illuminate.

In March 2015, PEW Research Center reported the results of their poll on the qualities important in a presidential candidate.[8] By an almost 2 to 1 margin, Republican voters said that "experience and a proven record" were more important than "new ideas and a different approach." But a mid-August poll by Fox[9] found Trump to be the front-runner in the Republican primary, doing more than twice as well as any other candidate. Three candidates who never held elected office, Trump (25 percent), Carson (12 percent), and Fiorina (5 percent), were the preferred candidates of 42 percent of Republican voters. If Ted Cruz (10 percent) with his two-year Senate career is added, a majority of Republican voters preferred one of the four candidates with little or no political experience to any of the 14 candidates with extensive experience and records.

People don't know what is important in their choice. Bad information is worse than no information. When the information is bad, we'll end up trying to solve the wrong problem.

If we shouldn't ask people why they do what they do, how do we find out the answer?

Unearthing True Motivations

We unearth "Why?" through observation or by simple analysis of people's responses to other questions. We can unearth why people do what they do and what might get them to change if we come at the question indirectly.

We can begin by making a list of the most likely reasons why some people already do what we would like our target to do. These people may choose candidate A over candidate B, or use brand C over brand D, or recycle aluminum cans instead of throwing them in the trash, or they may have already stopped smoking.

Read about the issue. Collect the best guesses of others. Learn about research that others have done into "Why?" unless that research simply asked a direct question. Even if our target is one person or a small group of people and we have no money for formal research, we can still do some informal research.

Talk to the people who already do what you'd like. Just don't ask them why they do what they do. Ask them what they think of the options. Ask them what they think of the people who do and don't do what you'd like. Observe people who choose candidate A, or use brand C, or recycle aluminum cans, or who have stopped smoking. Observe with an eye toward understanding the desires that seem to underlie their behavior.

On the basis of what you have found, what do you think motivates people who already behave the way you'd like? What reward do you think they associate with these actions? At this point, your suspicions about their motives will likely be a good deal more accurate than if you had asked them directly.

If you believe the same reward that motivates people who already behave the way you'd like would also motivate your target, you can begin building that association.

Let's say the action you seek is recycling aluminum cans and your target is a man who doesn't recycle. You conclude from your informal analysis that people who do recycle do so because recycling makes them feel they are contributing to a cleaner environment. If you believe that same reward would motivate your target, you can start to build that association.

If the reward that others seem to get from the action you suggest won't work for your target, you have to try something else. Continuing the recycling example, if the suggestion that he is contributing to a cleaner environment doesn't look like it will motivate him, you have to find another reward.

Ask yourself what your target wants that they can get by doing what you would like. Look at those two circles—target desires and action outcomes—and examine the overlap. What does your target want that can result from the action you recommend? Don't ask them what they want; observe. Ask others for their observations. Ask the target what they think of the options. Ask them what they think of the people who do and don't do what you'd like.

If your non-recycler wants to lower the cost of government and you can make the case that recycling lowers the cost of garbage disposal, you may have found a useful approach to persuasion. Now the challenge is to associate recycling with lower cost of garbage disposal and raise the salience of both ideas and there is a good chance your target will become a recycler.

"Saving the earth" might motivate most people who currently use CFLs (compact florescent bulbs), but won't motivate people who aren't yet using CFLs. Look more closely at what those people think who do use CFLs, but aren't interested in "saving the earth." You'll likely find that perceived efficiency is what motivates people who aren't worried about "saving the earth" and efficiency is the way to grow CFL use.

Deli Depot

Take a different case, one in which your target is many people. Let's say you have a fast food restaurant called Deli Depot, and you would like your customers to recommend Deli Depot to a friend.[10]

You begin the same way. Make a list of the most likely reasons why someone would recommend Deli Depot. Read about the issue. Collect the best guesses of others. Learn about research that others have done into "Why?" unless that research simply asked a direct question.

As a result of all your background work (market researchers would call this "secondary research"), you have six hypotheses about why a customer might recommend Deli Depot to a friend. You hypothesize that the perceived perceptions that matter are 1) excellent food quality, 2) competitive prices, 3) competent employees, 4) friendly employees, 5) wide variety of food, and 6) fast service.

In a survey, ask a couple hundred customers about their perceptions of Deli Depot on each of those attributes, as well as how likely they are to recommend Deli Depot to a friend. Fortunately, that's what the folks at Deli Depot did. In fact, they went further. In the same questionnaire, they also asked customers to rank the attributes from most important to least important in their fast food restaurant selection. The results are instructive.

Customers reported that "excellent food quality" followed by "competitive prices" are the most important criteria in their fast food restaurant selection. However, if you tried to guess how likely a person was to recommend Deli Depot to a friend knowing only their rating of Deli Depot on "excellent food quality" or "competitive prices," you couldn't do a very good job. You could do a much better job guessing how likely a person was to recommend Deli Depot to a friend if you knew only their rating of the restaurant on "friendly employees" or "competent employees."

Reported importance—what people say is important—is very different from what is actually related to recommending Deli Depot to a friend. This is pretty common. When asked to consciously evaluate importance, people give the answer that appears most rational. But what really influences preference is often experiential qualities like friendly employees.

Of course, people care about "excellent food quality" and "competitive prices." But Deli Depot and the other options people thought about were probably all good enough on "excellent food quality" and "competitive prices," and small differences on those attributes were not very predictive of whether a person would recommend Deli Depot to a friend.

As we all know, a connection between a perception and likelihood of recommending Deli Depot doesn't mean the perception caused the likelihood of recommendation. Correlation doesn't mean causality. However, the absence of a connection, the absence of correlation, does mean that the perception in question has little persuasive value. You can use the lack of correlation to eliminate perceptions that don't matter.

Look at the perceptions people hold that are related to whether they will or will not do what you'd like. If a perception is unrelated to what people do, that perception isn't causing the behavior.

Take "speed of service" as an example. "Speed of service" is not directly related to the likelihood of recommending Deli Depot to a friend if:

1. The perception truly doesn't matter. If people who say the service is fast and people who say the service is slow are equally likely to recommend Deli Depot, the perception of fast service doesn't matter.

2. Few people hold that perception or its opposite. If almost no one says the service is fast or if almost everyone says the service is fast, the perception of fast service can't explain why a sizable group of people are likely to recommend Deli Depot and another sizable group of people aren't.

3. The perception has a more complicated relationship with likelihood of recommendation. A more complicated relationship would exist if people who think Deli Depot's service is very fast and people who think Deli Depot's service is very slow are both likely to recommend Deli Depot, whereas people who think Deli Depot's service is neither particularly fast nor particularly slow are unlikely to recommend Deli Depot.

Whether (1), (2), or (3) holds, the perception of fast service is of little persuasive value. So the absence of correlation can be used to whittle down the list of possibilities.

When a perception, such as the perception of friendly employees, is correlated to likelihood of recommending Deli Depot to a friend, we still need to look further. If a perception is related to what people do, it *might* be the explanation. But you should ask yourself:

- Are both the perception and the behavior caused by some third variable?

- Is causality reversed with the behavior causing the perception?

- Are you looking at a halo effect?

If the survey sample was small and included many relatives of employees, those relatives might say both that the employees are friendly and they themselves are likely to recommend Deli Depot to a friend. The correlation you see could be caused by this third variable: respondent relationship. It should be easy for Deli Depot management to confirm that their respondents were indeed a random sample of patrons by making sure that employees didn't know when the survey would be conducted and didn't have any influence over respondent selection.

If causality is reversed, likelihood of recommending Deli Depot causes people to perceive employees as friendly rather than the other way around. It's not likely, but worth considering.

The "halo" effect would suggest that if we like something, we believe a wide range of positive things about it even if we don't have evidence for those positive things. But if one or two positive perceptions are related to likelihood of recommending Deli Depot and the others are not, then the halo effect does not explain what we see.

Customers who perceive Deli Depot employees as friendly and competent are more likely to recommend Deli Depot to a friend. Despite what people say about the importance of "excellent food quality" and "competitive prices," customers' perceptions of Deli Depot on those attributes are less related to likelihood of recommending Deli Depot. Under current conditions, a small gain in perceived friendly and competent employees is likely to make a bigger difference in recommendation than a small gain in perceived food quality and competitive prices. If we are trying to increase recommendations, it is clear where we should put the emphasis.

The idea that the best way to increase recommendations of Deli Depot is to increase the perception that Deli Depot employees are friendly and competent is unexpected, provocative, and true.

A couple of additional cases should clarify how it is possible to unearth the real reason "Why?"

Discover Card

This example of the unearthing process comes from when Discover Card was a relatively new credit card.

At that time, many people had a Discover Card in their wallet, but use of the card was still low. Management wanted people who already had a Discover Card in their wallet to pull the Discover Card out first, that is, make it their preferred credit card.

We began by making a list of the most likely explanations for preference for Discover Card among people who already had a Discover Card. We came up with several possibilities. Here are some:

- Low annual percentage rate. People who prefer Discover Card associate it with a low APR.

- Low annual fee. People who prefer Discover Card associate it with a low annual fee.

- Wide acceptance. People who prefer Discover Card believe it is widely accepted by merchants.

- Classy image. People who prefer Discover Card associate it with a classy image or, at least, not a blue-collar image. (Discover Card was originated by Sears and it was feared the working class Sears image was holding the card back.)

- Savings plan. People who prefer Discover Card realize Discover Card offers a savings account.

- Cash back. People who prefer Discover Card associate it with cash back on purchases. This was in the days before "cash back" became a popular credit card attribute.

We surveyed people who already had a Discover Card and asked their perceptions of the card and their credit card preference. We looked to see which perception of Discover Card was related to preference for Discover Card.

The proportion of people who made Discover Card their preferred card was the same among those who thought Discover Card had a low APR as it was among people who did not and the same among people who thought Discover Card had a low annual fee as it was among people who did not. The proportion of people who made Discover Card their preferred card was actually lower among people who thought the card was widely accepted. Apparently, people who preferred the card had tried to use it more often and had more experience with rejection.

The proportion of people who made Discover Card their preferred card was about the same regardless of their perceptions of the image of card users. The proportion of people who preferred Discover

Card was about the same among those who thought Discover Card offers a savings account as among people who did not.

The only perception that was positively associated with preference was "cash back." People who associated Discover Card with "cash back" were much more likely than others to make Discover Card their preferred card. After talking to people who didn't yet prefer Discover Card about the idea of getting cash back, we decided that "cash back" was an association that would also motivate them. In retrospect, this may seem obvious. At the time, it came as a revelation. Previous advertising for Discover Card talked about a laundry list of rewards, unable to decide what was most important.

We recommended a program of communication that dropped everything else and focused exclusively on "cash back." We wanted to build an automatic association between Discover Card and "cash back." It worked. Discover Card grew six-fold in seven years.

Cheese

Promoting cheese is another example of unearthing "Why?" rather than asking "Why?" Why do some people serve cheese more often than others? You may think you know the answer, but you probably don't.

We were trying to win the job of advertising cheese on behalf of the National Dairy Board (NDB). We assumed that getting people who reject cheese to start serving cheese would be tough. We decided instead to try to get women who only occasionally serve cheese to their family to serve it more often. Among people who serve cheese to their family, we wondered what explained how often they served it. Along with the National Dairy Board, we had a number of hypotheses:

1. Perceived nutritional benefits of cheese. Women who serve cheese only occasionally have a lower perception of the nutritional benefits of cheese (calcium, protein)

than women who serve cheese frequently; that is, they don't automatically associate cheese with its nutritional benefits.

2. Perceived nutritional drawbacks of cheese. Women who serve cheese only occasionally have a higher concern about the nutritional drawbacks (calories, fat) of cheese than women who serve cheese frequently.

3. Perceived cost of cheese. Women who serve cheese only occasionally see cheese as more expensive than women who serve cheese frequently.

4. Perceived taste of cheese. Women who serve cheese only occasionally have a less positive perception of the taste of cheese than women who serve cheese frequently.

5. Awareness of recipes using cheese. Women who serve cheese only occasionally can't think of as many simple recipes using cheese as women who serve cheese frequently.

We interviewed a lot of women who serve cheese to their families. We asked them how often they served cheese and a number of questions about their related perceptions and knowledge.

We found that women who occasionally served cheese and women who frequently served it had the same perception of its nutritional benefits and its nutritional drawbacks. Both types of women were enthusiastic about the benefits of cheese and not too concerned with the possible drawbacks.

We found that women who occasionally served cheese and women who frequently served it had the same perception of the cost and the taste of cheese. Both types of women felt that cheese was worth the price and both liked the taste.

What distinguished occasional cheese servers from frequent ones was awareness of easy to prepare recipes that use cheese. The less-frequent cheese servers couldn't think of many simple ways to serve it. This fit with another fact we had gathered: women who only occasionally served cheese were less confident and less experienced cooks than women who often served it. The real reason some women were serving cheese less often than others was not nutrition, taste, or cost, but the availability in their mind of simple serving suggestions.

We recommended that the advertising be used to give women those very simple serving suggestions. The NDB took our recommendation. The advertising, for example, said that adding a little melted cheese could make broccoli "disappear" and turn peas into "whoopeas." It worked. The "Don't forget the cheese" campaign got occasional cheese servers to serve it more often and, to our pleasant surprise, also got frequent cheese servers to serve it more often. Increasing the availability of easy cheese recipes encouraged all cheese servers to serve it more often.

If we had directly asked occasional and frequent cheese servers why they served it as often as they did, we would have gotten answers that made complete sense to the respondents and to us. But the answers may have had little to do with the real basis of behavior and we likely would have set off to solve the wrong problem.

The cheese experience also highlights the importance of aiming at the act rather than the attitude. Attitude wasn't holding people back. The target had a positive attitude toward cheese—its nutrition, price, and taste. What was holding people back was the availability of easy serving suggestions. When we made those easy serving suggestions available, the lizard's behavior changed.

Don't ask people why they do what they do, or how they choose, or what's most important in their decision. People don't know the answer, but they think they do. Bad information is worse than no information.

Unearth the answer with some basic research, whether informal or formal. See what people who already act as you would like associate with the behavior you seek. Decide whether the same association would also motivate your target. If so, begin to build the association. If not, find something else in the overlap of what your target wants and the possible outcomes of the action you propose. Build that association.

People don't intentionally mislead us. They just are convinced they know why they do what they do when they really have no idea. As Rogers and Hammerstein said, "Who can tell you why? Fools give you reasons. Wise men never try." [11]

The shrewd don't ask. They unearth.

7

FOCUS ON FEELING

D r. Spock of *Star Trek* is the cultural icon of clear thinking because he feels no emotion.

But, to our surprise, we recently found that emotions are critical to rational decision-making. Without emotions, we would be less rational and we would make poorer decisions.

The foremost expert on the role of emotion in decision-making is Antonio Damasio, head of the department of neurology at the University of Iowa College of Medicine in Iowa City. The research of Damasio and his team has shown that emotions play a critical role in making the right decisions.

People who lose the ability to feel emotion make poorer choices. Certain emotions, rather than clouding rational decision-making, are actually essential to it.

Damasio described his subjects who lost the ability to feel emotion like this: "Their ability to tackle the logic of a problem remains intact. Nonetheless, many of their personal and social decisions are irrational, more often disadvantageous to their selves and to others than not."[1]

An experiment, partially described in Chapter 1, illustrated the importance of emotion to decision-making. In that experiment,

Damasio and his colleagues demonstrated that our nonconscious, automatic mental system is capable of "Deciding Advantageously Before Knowing the Advantageous Strategy." [2] The experiment involved a simulated gambling task. The scientists asked participants to turn over cards from one of four decks placed before them. Most of the time, turning over a card led to a reward, but occasionally, and unpredictably, a card led to a loss. Two of the decks were more risky than the others, but participants had no way of knowing that. Participants began to avoid the risky decks shortly after the experiment began, even before they consciously knew which decks were risky. Their perspiration revealed that these participants began to feel emotionally uncomfortable whenever they thought about choosing a card from a risky deck even before they consciously knew it was a risky choice. The automatic, nonconscious mental system sensed risk before the reflective system was conscious of it. The automatic system communicated that risk and influenced choice through emotion.

Unmentioned in Chapter 1 was that the study also included a set of participants who were patients with a type of brain damage that made them unable to feel emotion. These participants, who could not feel emotion, never began to avoid the riskier decks even though they went through the same procedure as the normal subjects.

The lizard uses emotions to arrive at its preferences and to guide decisions. That reliance on emotion may make those decisions more, not less "rational." A focus on feelings need not lead to irrationality.

We usually answer the question of what people want with an attribute. People want lower prices, fewer calories, more lanolin, faster processing, or happy kids. And people do indeed want those things. However, it is often useful to take things up a level, working from an attribute toward the way that attribute makes us feel. The lizard inside responds more to the emotion of how the attribute makes us feel rather than to the attribute itself.

Show People How to Feel the Way They Would Like to Feel

The recommendation that we "show people how to get what they want" can often be rephrased as "show people how to feel the way they would like to feel."

Working up from attributes to feelings is a process sometimes called laddering. I want faster processing on my electronic device because then I don't have to wait. When I don't have to wait, I can accomplish more. When I accomplish more, I feel more in charge. I feel more powerful.

The most ordinary of attributes can ladder to a desirable feeling.

Shasta is a regional soft drink generally a lot less expensive than national brands like Coke, Pepsi, 7-Up, or Dr. Pepper. And, unlike national brands, which each come in a predominant single flavor, Shasta comes in a variety of flavors—orange, grape, root beer, cola, lemon/lime, and so on.

We found that variety of flavors is an attribute that can be laddered. Variety is inherently more interesting than monotony. Because of its variety of flavors, Shasta can be more fascinating, and when we choose a variety of flavors we ourselves can feel more fascinating.

The creative team of Emerson and Werme translated the attribute of variety of flavors into feeling more interesting with lyrics that described Coke and Pepsi as the "so-so soda" and the "same old cola" and Shasta as a "rock and rola." The lyrics were sung with rock and roll accompaniment and colorful visuals.

Shasta management decided before long that Shasta's real advantage was its low price and Shasta's price advantage was communicated convincingly at the shelf. After a short run, the advertising was discontinued. However, 30 years after those commercials aired, people still go online to reminisce about the ads and recall the lyrics still bouncing around inside their head.

The Shasta ads are not an example of marketplace success. But the Shasta ads do illustrate how the choice between possibly the world's leading brand and a minor brand can be laddered up to a choice of feelings—"same old cola" vs. "rock and rola."

When we take the reward from an attribute up to a feeling, we gain a number of advantages.

When we focus on feeling, we gain impact because we translate a rational reward into an emotional reward.

We shouldn't leave the translation up to the target because the target may not make it. Gore-Tex means waterproof. Waterproof means more comfort outdoors. More comfort outdoors means more fun camping. The attribute is only a means to an end. The end, what our target really wants, is the feeling. The feeling that we'll have more fun camping can be experienced even if we never actually go camping. Gore-Tex is a reason to believe that the anticipation of more fun camping will follow from purchase. The feeling of anticipating more fun camping is more motivating than the attribute of waterproof.

Match Light charcoal is another example of gaining impact by laddering up from an attribute to a feeling, from a rational reward to an emotional reward.

Match Light charcoal is "instant light" charcoal. Instant light charcoal already has lighter fluid in it. Nothing need be added. You can just light it with a match and the instant light charcoal will do the rest. Regular charcoal, like Kingsford, requires using lighter fluid or a charcoal chimney.

With regular charcoal, successful lighting is not difficult but not guaranteed. You might not use enough lighter fluid and the charcoal won't get going. You might use too much lighter fluid and end up with an unanticipated blaze. If you use a charcoal chimney, the charcoal in that chimney might go out before it is sufficiently lit, leaving your guests waiting for those steaks.

Instant light charcoal is more convenient. It saves a step or two and nothing extra is needed.

Associating Match Light with convenience seemed the obvious way to go. But the people working on Match Light wondered if they could get more impact by laddering up from the attribute of convenience to a feeling. They found that people who use instant light charcoal differed from people who use regular charcoal in consistent ways. People who use instant light charcoal are worriers. They tend to worry more about all sorts of things. They worry more about money. They worry more about their job. They worry more about their kids. They worry more about their appearance, and so on. The Match Light team realized their brand could offer these worriers not just convenience, but confidence and freedom from worry. The Match Light team translated the attribute of convenience into a feeling that was both what people who buy instant light charcoal want and what Match Light can provide.

When we focus on feeling, we also have more control. The target might translate an attribute into a feeling other than the one we want to offer as a reward. Choosing a product with the attribute of "low fat" can translate into feeling healthy, feeling sexy, or feeling like a good parent. When we craft our persuasion, we can pick the feeling that is the most powerful reward to associate with that choice. When we do the translation from attribute into feeling, we gain precision.

Ease in finding a job or a higher salary are attributes that might serve as rewards if we are trying to get our teen to stay in school. Our pitch will be more persuasive if we ladder those attributes up to a feeling. Our teen might ladder those attributes up to feeling of recognition or the feeling of pride. But getting a job and a better salary can also ladder to a feeling of independence. If we have learned that this teen really wants to feel independent, we should do the translation. We should focus on the feeling of independence and direct the laddering gaining precision.

When we focus on feeling, we not only translate a rational reward into an emotional reward, we also translate a delayed and uncertain reward into one that is more immediate and certain. This is critical because, as we saw, actions that are good for us often have delayed and uncertain rewards.

According to most economic models, the appeal of a benefit declines exponentially with time. Research on the issue suggests that the actual appeal of a benefit declines hyperbolically with time. That means that the appeal of a reward declines with time even more rapidly than originally thought. Lately, George Loewenstein, the Herbert A. Simon professor of economics and psychology at Yale, has studied what he calls visceral rewards (food for a hungry person, sex for an amorous person, sleep for a sleepy person, and so on) and has discovered that the attraction of these visceral rewards declines more rapidly still.[3] When it comes to visceral rewards, our present bias is even more pronounced and the immediate is even more appealing relative to the delayed. Along with delay often comes some loss of certainty. Any salesman knows that a sale delayed is a less certain sale.

A persuasion attempt becomes more powerful when we focus on feeling and transform a reward that is delayed, uncertain, and rational into one which is immediate, certain, and emotional.

Consuming milk contributes to strong bones. But bone strength is a reward that is delayed, uncertain, and rational. Strong bones are a long way off. A glass of milk doesn't guarantee strong bones. And strong bones, if they do arrive, are a fact not a feeling. Even if strong bones are a long way off and not guaranteed, I can feel healthy right now. We can transform the delayed, uncertain, and rational reward of strong bones into the immediate, certain, and emotional reward of feeling healthy.

Choosing carrots instead of a candy bar can contribute to weight loss. But weight loss is a long way off. Right now, a candy bar will taste better than carrots. But, when I choose the carrots, I can feel virtuous right away even though I won't become thin for a while if ever. The delayed, uncertain, and rational reward of weight loss can be transformed into the immediate, certain, and emotional reward of feeling virtuous.

Stopping smoking can help me avoid cancer. But cancer is probably a long way off and avoiding cancer is by no means certain. Right now, a cigarette would surely be a lot more enjoyable than no cigarette. Even if the reward of avoiding cancer is delayed and uncertain, I can feel right now like a good father who is doing what he can to be there for his kids. The delayed, uncertain, and rational reward of avoiding cancer can be transformed into the immediate, certain, and emotional reward of feeling like a good father.

When we translate an attribute into a feeling, we turn a delayed, uncertain, often rational reward into a reward that is much more motivating to the lizard, our automatic, nonconscious mental system.

When we focus on feeling, we gain power.

How will it feel to quit smoking? How will it feel to stay on that diet? How will it feel to stay in school and work toward a good job and independence? How will it feel to drive a new hybrid car or to drive a new muscle car?

Tell whomever you are trying to persuade how it will feel when they take your recommended option

- Because feelings are what they really want.
- Because the physical reward may be delayed, but the feeling is immediate.
- Because the physical reward may be uncertain, but the feeling is assured.
- Because a fact or a feature is rational, but a feeling is emotional and speaks to the automatic mind.

When someone donates to help save an endangered species, the result is delayed, uncertain, and rational. If their donation makes the donor feel like a defender of wildlife, the result is immediate, certain, and emotional.

There is another reason to translate an attribute into a feeling. When we focus on feeling, we can tap into an additional class of rewards that doesn't depend on the physical experience of the action we recommend.

Actor Image

Many feelings do flow from the physical experience of an action. The indulgent feeling of a spoonful of creamy, full-fat ice cream and the feeling of excitement that comes from driving a car that has great acceleration are examples of feelings that depend on the physical experience.

But some feelings don't come from physical experience. Feeling more masculine when smoking a certain brand of cigarette doesn't come from the physical experience. Feeling more fit when wearing shoes with a particular logo doesn't result from the physical experience. Feeling more masculine or feeling more fit comes from image enhancement and image enhancement does not depend on physical experience. It only depends on our perception of people who perform that action—actor image. Actor image is the stereotype of people who perform a particular action and actor image can be a powerful tool in persuasion. The lizard infers the attractiveness of the action we recommend from the people it associates with that action.

We have an image of people who have stopped smoking, drive a Toyota, wear Nike, or reject drugs. The actor image may be sharply defined, like the perception of people who own a Rolls Royce, or vague, like the perception of people who live in the St. Louis metropolitan area. It may be accurate or it may be inaccurate. But, when we perform an action, we, to some degree, identify with that actor image. When we buy fresh produce, we clothe ourselves in the stereotype of people who do likewise. If the actor image is sufficiently attractive to us, we are drawn to perform that action because we are pleased to be seen as one of those people. If the actor image is unattractive, we are embarrassed to perform that action.

Because feelings are invisible, they can be hard to communicate. Actor image can make feelings visible. The people who already act as you would like them to act are, in a sense, a club that your target joins if your target also acts as you recommend. By taking your recommended option, your target gets to feel like a member of that club. If guys who drink the Budweiser seem manly, your target feels manly when they drink it. If women who wear Victoria's Secret seem sexy, your target feels sexy when they wear it.

Actor image or user image has long been a staple of professional marketing, but actor image works in personal persuasion as well. What can you do to show your teen that those who don't do drugs are cool and fun? Teens who perceive those who reject drugs as cool, independent, fun, and intelligent are likely to reject drugs themselves. Teens who perceive those who reject drugs as boring, under the thumb of adults, party poopers, and nerds are embarrassed to reject drugs, and we have a problem.

Image enhancement comes in two closely related forms: public image enhancement and self-image enhancement. In public image enhancement, we enjoy feeling that others see us as we would like to be seen. In self-image enhancement, we enjoy feeling we are the sort of person we would like to be.

Public Image Enhancement

We societal animals are designed to seek social approval in the form of affection or esteem. We want to feel that others like us or that others think we are fun, smart, sexy, competent, good-looking, fashionable, and on and on.

When we buy fresh produce, we assume that people see us as one of those people who buy fresh produce. We believe the actions we take influence how others see us. The "spotlight effect"[4] is a label scientists have given to our exaggerated notion of how much our actions influence others' perception of us. We tend to think that everybody is noticing us when, in fact, most are ignoring us.

Our action can make us feel that others see us as we would like to be seen or our action can make us uncomfortable, fearing that others see us as we would not like to be seen.

As persuaders, we can associate buying a bag of oranges in the grocery store with the feeling that others will see us as a good parent. With effort, we can help people feel proud to put a bag of oranges on the checkout counter and embarrassed to put a bag Cheetos on the checkout counter.

Self-Image Enhancement

Sometimes when we take an action, we can enjoy participating in the image of the actor whether or not anyone else is aware of what is happening. It can be a pleasure to clothe our self in the image of one who buys fresh produce, drives a Cadillac, or smokes a Marlboro, and that pleasure doesn't require the perceptions of others. A person can enjoy feeling masculine by smoking a Marlboro cigarette even if nobody else is around. Parents can feel like good parents when preparing oatmeal for their child even when no one else is aware of what is being served. Self-image enhancement can occur without public image enhancement.

Image enhancement is a reward that has broad implications because actor image is rich in associations.

The lizard, our automatic, nonconscious mind, works through association—any concept calls to mind other concepts which in turn call to mind still other concepts. Some concepts have broader implications. They result in wider association and cause greater inference. Actor image is a concept with broad implications.

As social animals, we naturally think in terms of people, stereotypes, and exemplars. They are critical to our ability to make sense of the world. We have a special skill at anticipating how other people will act based on what we know about them. We even personify inanimate objects like cars and computers in order to help us antic-ipate or explain their behavior.

Actor image will often tell people more about an action we rec-ommend than anything we say.

If we want voters to vote for our candidate, if we want our spouse to stop smoking, if we want our teen to stay in school, it's helpful to adjust our target's stereotype of people who do what we suggest. A positive actor image generalizes and makes our candidate seem far more appealing in more ways than we have time to explain. A pos-itive actor image of a nonsmoker makes it much easier for a smoker to consider quitting. A positive actor image can give our teen more reasons to stay in school than we ourselves can even imagine.

If we are selling cars, actor image can be one of our most power-ful tools. Prospective buyers have a hard time comparing the options in any objective way. Who really understands the technology of the modern automobile? Even "experts" disagree on quality and value.

For most people, choosing a car is a leap of faith. How do peo-ple decide where to put their faith? The technology is unfathomable. People realize they are not good judges of the physical qualities of a car, but they believe they are good judges of the people who buy that car. People judge the qualities of a car by their perception of the qualities of the people associated with it. Within obvious finan-cial restraints, they will choose the car that matches the person they would like to be. If they would like to see themselves as smart, they'll choose a car that they perceive smart people drive. If they would like to see themselves as stylish, they'll choose a car that they think styl-ish people drive. And so on.

The salesperson's job is to figure out who the buyer would like to be and help him or her find the car that makes them feel that way. To be most successful, the salesperson should embody the qualities that people considering the car seem to be seeking—smartness, stylish-ness, assertiveness, or whatever. As we know, the salesperson doesn't have to actually be smart, stylish, or assertive; he or she just has to act that way. In the eyes of prospective buyers, you are what you do no matter why you do it.

Westin Hotels

Westin is an example of associating an action (staying at a Westin) with how business travelers want to feel and doing so through actor image.

When choosing a hotel, convenience is critical. But hotels are often clustered, so a variety of hotels are equally convenient for the traveler and something other than convenience must serve as the basis of choice. Is it the expected comfort of the bed, the expected cleanliness of the room, the expected responsiveness of the staff, or the quality of the expected restaurant and bar?

With hotels, we found that the most important factor was the perception of the sort of guests who stay there.

Westin Hotels are much like other hotels in the same price range—Hilton, Hyatt, Sheraton. They are clean. Beds are comfortable. Service is prompt. The hotel restaurant and bar are enjoyable.

We surveyed frequent business travelers, asking their perceptions of each hotel chain on a variety of dimensions like cleanliness, comfort, service, amenities, and so on. We also asked their hotel preference, assuming all hotels were equally convenient to their destination. We then looked at the connection between business travelers' perceptions of hotels in this price range and preference for hotels in this price range. We found that one perception stood out. Perceptions of cleanliness, comfort, service, and so on were of little use in predicting a business traveler's hotel preference. But when business travelers perceived that one hotel had an advantage on "for sophisticated travelers," they were four times more likely to make that hotel their first choice. Hotel preference was much more closely connected with "for sophisticated travelers" than with any other perception. As with beer brand choice, social, emotional rewards were more motivating than rational, physical rewards.

Associating the Westin guest with a sophisticated traveler held a lot of promise. We talked to a lot of business travelers, enough to know that they want others to see them as sophisticated and that they want to see themselves in the same way. The idea that Westin guests are sophisticated travelers has broad implications; that is, it is a concept that is rich with meaning. If Westin guests are sophisticated travelers, then Westin must have comfortable beds, responsive service, and a quality restaurant. On the other hand, the idea that Westin has comfortable beds is a narrow concept, one that is not rich with meaning. "Comfortable beds" does not imply that Westin has responsive service and a quality restaurant and does not suggest that Westin guests are sophisticated.

We felt we could increase preference for Westin if we could build an association between staying at Westin and feeling like a sophisticated traveler. That turned out to be right. We showed the frequent traveler how to feel like a sophisticated traveler. All they had to do was choose Westin. A campaign was designed that featured an almost insufferably sophisticated man or almost insufferably sophisticated woman and asked the provocative question, "Who's he/she sleeping with?" The question, of course, was quickly answered with "Westin." Immediately after the campaign began airing, reservations through the reservation system started to climb. About a year later, the investment firm that had recently purchased the Westin chain was able to sell it for a billion more than they paid for it.

When we focus on a feeling rather than an attribute, we:

- Gain the power of promising an end rather than a means.
- Gain precision because, without guidance, an attribute can lead to many different feelings.
- Turn a delayed, uncertain, and rational benefit into an immediate, certain, and emotional reward.

- Tap into an additional class of rewards that doesn't depend on the physical experience of the action we recommend—actor image rewards.

When we promise the feeling of participating in an attractive actor image, we:

- Offer our target the opportunity to appear to others as the person they would like to be—public image enhancement.

- Offer our target the opportunity to appear to themselves as the person they would like to be—self-image enhancement.

- Imply a variety of positive qualities of the action naturally associated with that actor image. Actor image is a concept that is rich with meaning.

8

CREATE EXPERIENCE
WITH EXPECTATION

What if we could make carrots taste better without changing carrots in any way?

What if we could make voting more fulfilling without doing anything to voting conditions?

What if we could make driving a new Ford Mustang more thrilling without changing anything in Mustang manufacturing?

We can.

What we see, feel, taste, or smell depends to a great degree on what we expect to see, feel, taste, or smell. Art historian Ernst Gombrich tells us that no eye is "innocent."[1] What the eye sees depends, only in part, on what is there to be seen. What the eye sees also depends on what it expects to see. No eye, no sense, is without expectation.

Our mind does not use sensory data alone to create our perceptions. Our mind combines input from our senses with our ideas about the world and past knowledge to create our perceptions. The physical characteristics of the stimulus contribute to perception through what psychologists call bottom-up mental processing. Expectations and prior knowledge contribute to perception through what psychologists call top-down mental processing. What we experience about the outside world is a result of both.

Perception is an unconscious process carried out by the lizard inside, our automatic mental system. Expectation guides perception.

Without expectation, perception is much slower. The influence of expectation on perception is an advantage for us humans because expectation speeds up the process of perception and allows us to more quickly approach pleasure or avoid pain. Expectation steers perception unless the stimulus is substantially unlike the expectation.

Different expectations and prior knowledge can lead to very different perceptions of the exact same thing.

12
A 13 C
14

Reading down, the figure in the middle of this set is clearly 13. Reading across, the figure in the middle is clearly B.

We see what we expect to see. If we change the expectation, we can change the experience. If we expect a carrot to taste a little better, it will. It won't taste completely differently, but it will taste a little better.

Thomas N. Robinson is a doctor with the department of pediatrics, Stanford Prevention Research Center, Department of Medicine. Dr. Robinson and his colleagues, in a carefully controlled experiment, gave children, aged 3 1/2 to 5 1/2, two separate servings of five different foods—hamburger, chicken nuggets, french fries, 1-percent milk, and baby carrots.[2] The research assistant who presented the food to the child sat behind a screen that separated him or her from the child. The child saw an arm reach around the screen to present each food, but the child could not see the body or face connected to the arm. The procedure must have been a little creepy for the child, though equally creepy with both test food and control food. For each food, one serving was packaged as from McDonald's and the other was similarly packaged, but unbranded. In each case, the McDonald's labeled food and the unlabeled food were actually identical.

For all five foods, the children said the food labeled as from McDonald's tasted better. In four out of five cases, all but the hamburger, the children's preference for McDonald's labeled food was highly significant. The McDonald's label created an expectation of better taste that influenced the children's experience. McDonald's labeled carrots tasted a little better than other carrots even though the carrots were physically the same. The children responded that way not because they are children, but because they are human.

For adults as well, the experience is different depending on the expectation.

Working for Anheuser-Busch, we traveled around the country talking to beer drinkers. They would often tell us that drinking a large quantity of certain brands of beer would give them headaches, but drinking a large quantity of other brands of beer would not. We noticed the brands of beer that were reported to give people headaches in one market were not the same as the brands reported to give people headaches in another market. The pattern became clear. The unpopularity of a brand in a market seemed to cause the headaches, rather than its chemical content. If Busch, for example, was unpopular in a market, beer drinkers described Busch as a brand that, in quantity consumption, caused headaches. On the other hand, if Busch was popular in that market, beer drinkers described Busch as a brand that did not cause headaches.

A beer drinker expects headaches from drinking a large quantity of an unpopular brand of beer and he gets them. A beer drinker does not expect headaches from drinking a large quantity of a popular brand of beer, and he experiences and remembers less discomfort from that consumption.

If we expect voting to be a little more fulfilling, it will. If we expect driving a Mustang to be a little more thrilling, it will. If we expect using public transportation to be a little more enjoyable, it will.

Unlabeled Coke vs. Labeled Coke

Samuel McClure is a member of the department of Psychology at Stanford University and director of Stanford's Decision Neuroscience Laboratory. McClure, et al.[3] measured the preference and brain activity of people drinking colas, both labeled and unlabeled. They found that people preferred the taste of labeled Coke to the same product unlabeled. No big surprise there. The surprise lay in the brain activity. They found that several areas of the brain "respond preferentially" to brand-cued Coke. In other words, even though the physical characteristics of the beverage were identical, the brain reacted differently when the beverage was labeled "Coke."

The experience of drinking labeled Coke was different from the experience of drinking unlabeled Coke, not in an imaginary way, or an illusory way, but in a real way. Expectation is capable of changing the way the brain responds. Expectation is capable of changing the chemistry of experience.

As Leonard Lee[4] from Columbia Business School and his colleagues point out, evidence that food expectations affect perception is plentiful, whether it's sliced turkey, seltzer water, beer, nutrition bars, coffee, strawberry yogurt, cheese spreads, or ice cream (Makens[5], Nevid[6], Allison and Uhl[7], Wansink, Park, Sonka, and Morganosky[8], Olson and Dover[9], Wardle and Solomons[10], Bowen, Tomoyasu, Anderson, Carney, and Kristal[11]).

Keith Reinhard, a member of the Advertising Hall of Fame and chairman emeritus of the marketing communications firm of DDB Worldwide, is fond of saying "Advertising is the last step in the manufacturing process." He means that the pleasure of consuming the product is due not only to the objective qualities built into the product in manufacturing, but also to the expectations attached to the product through marketing communication.

We can enhance our children's pleasure in eating a vegetable dish by enhancing their expectation. We, of course, shouldn't over-promise. But we can lead them to expect something of the pleasure we get by eating that dish. We can change their experience by changing their expectation.

Extended Stay America gave us a great example of what not to do. They believed that people want to feel at home at a hotel. So they created a commercial in which their guests felt so comfortable, so at home at Extended Stay America, that they felt free to pass gas whenever they wanted. The commercial modified experience with expectation, but probably not the modification Extended Stay America wanted. The ad led potential guests to expect they would get a room at Extended Stay America in which the previous guest was freely farting.

Westin Hotels, on the other hand, created the expectation of a hotel that is preferred by sophisticated travelers. Westin guests not only expected a better experience, they had a better experience because they tended to notice anything that a sophisticated traveler might like.

In most cases simple affect guides our expectations, preferences, and decisions. We go with what we like. Our mind tags representations of things (people, objects, actions), as Slovic, et al.[12] would say, with a degree of positive or negative affect that summarizes the impressions we have of those things. In the future, we may not consciously recall the impression, but the affect, the liking, remains.

It doesn't take much liking to steer our choices. It has been demonstrated that we feel mildly positively or negatively about certain cities, states, products, and technologies. Liking has a strong influence on preference even if we don't know why we like what we like.

Slight differences in liking tend to become magnified. We seek out, notice, and pay attention to information that supports our current perspective. We pay little attention to evidence that contradicts our current perspective. This well-known bias is usually referred to as selective exposure. When information gets through our selective screen, we don't treat it objectively. We interpret the information in a way that supports what we already believe. This is usually referred to as selective perception. People with different perspectives on the way things work can interpret the same data in two radically different ways. Almost any event in political news will be interpreted by liberals as supporting a liberal worldview and by conservatives as supporting a conservative worldview. Together, selective exposure and selective perception make up "confirmation bias."[13] We all exhibit confirmation bias, lay people and scientists alike.

If we feel a little more positively about a certain action, whether that action is voting for candidate A, not experimenting with drugs, buying fresh produce, or not having a cigarette, we seek out evidence that reinforces that feeling and ignore evidence that doesn't. Confirmation bias doesn't require much affect, just a hypothesis we are willing to entertain. If a fortune teller says that we will meet a handsome stranger, we notice evidence that might confirm that prediction and ignore evidence that might disconfirm it. Confirmation bias no doubt contributes to the rise and persistence of superstition and the success of soothsayers of all stripes and makes it very difficult for liberals and conservatives to agree on anything, no matter what the objective data.

Our affection persists and grows due to confirmation bias. Our affection for an action, however minor, sets our expectation. Our expectation heavily influences our experience of that action.

If we can improve, even slightly, the affection we feel for an action, we can improve our expectation, and improve the experience of the action. If we can improve, even slightly, the affection we feel for eating carrots, we can make carrots taste a little better. If we can improve, even slightly, the affection we feel for driving a Mustang, we can make driving that Mustang a little more thrilling.

And if we can improve, even slightly, the affection we feel for an action, that affection becomes self-supporting through confirmation bias. People will seek out, notice, and pay attention to information that reinforces that affection. Other information is likely to be ignored.

How, then, do we increase affection? How do we make people a little fonder of the action we suggest?

Increasing affection is not as difficult as it may seem. Mere exposure can do it.

A long list of experiments demonstrates that repeated exposure to a stimulus increases our affection and preference for it.[14] The studies have shown that this happens with nonsense phrases, human faces, Chinese ideographs, and other visual stimuli. And it's not just visual stimuli. Repeated exposure reliably increases affection for sounds, tastes, abstract ideas, and social stimuli. The mere exposure effect even works in nonhuman species.

We don't need to pay attention. The stimulus needs no reinforcement. The exposure can be so subtle that we don't even realize that it occurred. Exposure to a stimulus, even without attention and reinforcement, increases our affection and preference for it.

Exposure works because the exposed stimulus becomes more mentally available to us. The lizard inside, our automatic system, is most influenced by, pays the most attention to, assumes the importance of, and has the most confidence in things and people that come most easily to mind.

In marketing, frequency of exposure and exposure relative to competing brands lead to brand awareness. Brand awareness is one measure of availability. And brand awareness has a powerful impact on choice.

Wayne Hoyer is Zale Centennial Fellow in retail merchandising and associate professor of marketing, University of Texas at Austin. Hoyer and Steven Brown[15] showed that when inexperienced consumers faced an unfamiliar brand choice task, brand awareness had a dramatic effect. Further, when given the opportunity to sample the products, consumers aware of one brand sampled fewer brands. Lastly, when aware of one brand in a choice set, consumers tended to choose the known brand even when it was of lower quality.

For the consumer, testing alternative brands is usually not feasible—impossible before purchase and difficult after purchase. Even in cases where the consumer can test competing brands, the results are often ambiguous because competing brands attempt to match each other on quality.

John Deighton is professor of business administration at Harvard Business School. Deighton suggests that when product testing is infeasible or ambiguous, consumers will withhold final judgment until trying the product.[16] But, he says, that consumer trial will not be a true product test. Rather, the small nudge of advertising and brand awareness combined with confirmation bias will affect how consumers conduct the test and how consumers interpret the experience, and will reinforce the small preference consumers had for the more familiar brand. This is exactly what Stephen Hoch and Young-Won Ha (University of Chicago's Graduate School of Business, Center of Decision Research) found.[17]

We can enhance the expectation of what it would be like to take the action we suggest, whether it's recycling an aluminum can or stopping smoking by increasing slightly our affection for that action. Mere exposure to the idea of that action can increase affection for it by making that action more available—that is, making that action come to mind more easily.

We can also enhance the expectation of what it would be like to take the action we suggest by improving the associations that come with that action. If our target wants to reduce the cost of government, and we are able to increase the association of recycling aluminum cans with lower cost of government through lower cost of garbage collection, we enhance the expectation. Imagine two situations in which the action of recycling aluminum cans is equally available. Imagine further that in the first situation, recycling is associated with lower cost of garbage collection and that association doesn't occur in the second situation. Chances of persuasion success in the first situation are much better.

When we can make the desired action come more easily to mind, we actually improve the experience by enhancing the expectation. When we go beyond availability and associate the desired action with attributes, feelings, or images that are rewarding to the target, we enhance the expectation and improve the experience even more.

With time, Marlboro cigarettes created two very different expectations of what it would be like to smoke a Marlboro.[18] These two different expectations resulted in two quite different experiences.

From the time of Queen Victoria until the 1950s, Phillip Morris positioned Marlboro as a women's cigarette using advertising lines such as "Marlboro—Mild as May." To enhance this position, Phillip Morris introduced an ivory-tipped version of Marlboro designed to stop bits of paper from sticking to the smoker's lips and later a red tipped version designed to hide lipstick smears. By the mid-1950s, Marlboro held only one quarter of 1 percent of the total domestic market.

In 1955, Phillip Morris reintroduced Marlboro as a filter cigarette with a new, now familiar, logo, a "flip-top" box, and a new positioning. No longer a women's cigarette, Phillip Morris sold Marlboro as a flavorful cigarette for ruggedly independent men. The ads associated Marlboro with manly users such as drill sergeants, construction workers, sailors, and, of course, cowboys, each holding the cigarette in a tattooed hand. In 1963, Marlboro fully committed to cowboys with theme music from the movie, *The Magnificent Seven*, western landscapes, and cowboy paraphernalia. The positioning and advertising have changed little since.

By the mid-1980s, Marlboro was the largest-selling cigarette brand in the world.

Before 1955, the experience of Marlboro was feminine. After 1955, the experience of Marlboro was masculine. The change in expectation changed the experience. Marlboro began behaving very differently. The actions of the brand overwhelmed former perceptions and led to the expectation of a masculine experience. The motive of the brand's behavior change was profit. But people drew inferences from the masculine behavior of Marlboro and ignored the circumstances that led to the behavior. For the lizard, you are what you do no matter why you do it.

Perception is an unconscious process carried out by the lizard inside, our automatic mental system. Expectation guides perception.

Don't wait. People's expectations will alter their experience. It is possible, but difficult, to change people's memory of an experience. It's easier to change up-front expectations and those, in turn, change the experience itself.

Before people do what you would like them to do, focus them on the positive qualities of the experience.

As we know, wine salesmen prepare people for the taste of a sip of wine. If left to their own devices, how many people would pick up on the nutty bouquet or hint of raspberry?

Parents' anticipation of and reaction to different foods change their children's experience and set their children's preferences. If you like the smell and taste of asparagus, let your children see your anticipation and reaction, and you improve the chances they will come to like asparagus.

You can make your partner's first experience with your extended family at Thanksgiving more pleasant by making him or her sensitive in advance to the amusing quirks and interesting aspects of the characters. If your partner senses dread on your part, he or she is in for a long evening.

You can completely change the outcome of a test drive by leading the driver to anticipate the positive aspects of the acceleration, braking, handling, and road feel. If you don't set the expectation beforehand, there is a good chance the driver will miss key selling points.

Of course, if you are selling a product, you owe it to your prospective customers to create positive expectations. Positive expectations are a big part of what customers are buying.

Naturally, it would be counterproductive to lead your target to anticipate outcomes that are factually inaccurate. Expecting 25 people to show up at a party when only 10 show up, or expecting acceleration from 0 to 60 in eight seconds when it takes 20 seconds, won't enhance the experience. But you can modify the interpretation of experience. The fun of the party is subjective not objective, and expecting fun is likely to make the experience more pleasant. The exhilaration one gets from acceleration is subjective, an internal interpretation of experience. The exhilaration the driver feels depends, in part, on how you set the driver's expectation.

When you set expectations, don't stop with the sensory. Go beyond senses to feelings. How will it feel to get good grades? How will it feel to order a Budweiser? How will it feel to not eat that piece of cake? Feelings are completely subjective, heavily dependent on expectation, and highly motivating.

Setting expectation has a long-term impact. It is persuasion with legs. Because expectation changes experience, your target may not only take your recommended option now, but is likely to choose it again and again.

We can change experience by changing expectation. We can make carrots taste a little better.

9

ADD A LITTLE ART

When we use communication to persuade, our chances of success are better if we add a little art—art of conversation, art of generating inference, and art of engagement. The lizard responds to art.

Art of Conversation

Dan Sperber and Deirdre Wilson, authors of the linguistics classic *Relevance: Communication and Cognition,* tell us that every time we send a message, even conversationally, we make a promise to the receiver.[1] We promise that he or she will want to receive the message we are sending. Any time we attempt to communicate with an audience of one or many, we make the tacit guarantee that they will find the message worthy of attention. The lizard automatically understands that promise and is disappointed if the promise is broken.

If a message only dully repeats what the receiver already knows for certain, it is not worthy of the receiver's attention.

Let's say our message is "You really should stop smoking." Our receiver likely already knows he or she should stop smoking and has heard that message a thousand times. The message "You really should stop smoking" violates our tacit guarantee and breaks our mutually understood promise that the message is worthy of the receiver's attention. The receiver lowers his or her expectation about what to expect from our future messages, and it becomes harder for us to reach and to persuade.

If you hope to persuade, have something interesting to say. By sending a message in whatever form, you are implicitly promising the receiver you have something to say they will want to hear. Don't break that promise.

Asking for behavior change while having nothing interesting to say is not persuasive.

Provide some new information or a new way of looking at the old information. Say what you have to say in a different, clever, or amusing way. Talk about something your target wants and show them how they can get it by doing what you ask. When you talk about something your target wants, there is a good chance they'll find what you say interesting.

Promising a receiver that he or she will want to receive our message is a high hurdle. Our normal tendency in persuasion is to create a message based on what we want to say with little regard to what the audience wants to receive.

Crafting a message that the receiver wants to get requires climbing inside the head of the receiver and understanding how the receiver looks at the world.

This is a complete turnaround. Rather than crafting a message by carefully honing what we want to say, we have to craft a message that the receiver will want to hear. If we break our promise, we take a big step backward in persuasion.

When attempting to be persuasive, how much of what parents say, of what spouses say, of what friends say fulfills the tacit guarantee of being a message the receiver will want to receive? Attempts at persuasion that fail to merit the attention of the audience are nagging.

In 2014, the Obama administration produced a Public Service Announcement to encourage people to enlist in the fight against sexual assault and to visit the Website, ItsOnUs.org. The public service announcement consisted largely of a variety of celebrities looking sternly into the camera and saying, "It's on us." The video is an example of nagging.

This message isn't concerned with what receivers want to hear, only with what the sender wants to say.

More than one-third of the people who expressed an opinion on this ad disliked it. It's clear from the comments that most of those who disliked the ad are in the ad's primary target, young men.

Why wouldn't this message work? Why would young men dislike an ad that literally says:

- "Stop sexual assault."
- "Don't blame the victim."
- "Get a friend home safe."

This message is not worthy of attention because it doesn't communicate what its target would like to hear. It only communicates what the sender wants to say.

Young men not only disliked this ad, it made them angry. Why?

The negative emotional reaction to the ad comes from its tone and style. What an ad says is less important than how the ad says it. The disapproving looks and somber music of the ad give the impression of parents wagging their fingers at sons who've disappointed them. The tone, style, and selection of spokespeople seem to communicate to many that young men are an embarrassment. That's not what the message literally says, but what an ad literally says and what an ad communicates are two different things.

It is possible to come at the problem in a different way.

One should start by thinking about what young men want that they can get by taking the anti-sexual assault pledge. For example, young men want to feel manly. They buy certain cigarettes to feel manly. They buy certain beers to feel manly. They wear certain clothes to feel manly. Can young men feel manly by taking the anti-sexual assault pledge? Of course they can. But young men won't feel manly by taking an apologetic, whiny "It's on us" pledge. If Danny Trejo, Robert De Niro, and Sylvester Stallone (or your favorite manly men) tell young men that "Real men don't" and encourage them to take the "Real men don't" pledge, many would take the pledge and few would get angry.

The "It's on us" message, as created, encourages people outside the target to pat themselves on the back for being against sexual assault. Unfortunately, it makes its target angry and doesn't do anything to reduce the problem. Talk about what young men want and show them how to get it. Make the message something young men want to hear, not something you want to say.

A persuasive message that fails to deliver on the promise of being worthy of attention is not just a disappointment, it's annoying.

Dale Carnegie's advice fits. "The only way on earth to influence people is to talk about what they want, and show them how to get it." If we are talking about what receivers want and showing them how to get it, receivers will be interested.

Sperber and Wilson have another piece of advice for us that might lead us to craft very different persuasive messages. Sperber and Wilson tell us that conversations work best when we leave out of the message anything receivers can and will provide on their own.

Being a receiver is an active, participatory job. Our audience will assume our message is one they want to receive. After all, that is our tacit guarantee. So our receivers will try to provide whatever details and context make our message relevant for them.

Herbert Paul Grice was a philosopher of language who revolutionized the study of meaning in communication. Grice spoke of "conversational implicatures." By that he meant "roughly, things that a hearer can work out from the way something was said rather than what was said."[2] To have the impact we desire, our communications should leave room for conversational implicatures—those thoughts provoked by the message and completed by the receiver.

In ordinary conversation, we are accustomed to leaving out everything receivers can provide on their own. We do it automatically and effortlessly. If I am at a party and a friend offers me a drink, I might say, "I'm driving." My response leaves out what my friend can fill in for himself, namely "No, I do not want a drink because I'm driving and I feel drinking might impair my ability to drive safely." If I had said all that, my friend would wonder why. He would likely feel patronized.

People take offense when we put too much in the message and underestimate their capacity to understand. If we include too much in our message, our audience will feel insulted and we forfeit our ability to persuade. But if we include too little, our message is unintelligible. If we strike the right balance, the audience feels we understand them and is more receptive. What's left out of a message establishes a degree of complicity, a level of emotional closeness between sender and the receiver.

Don't communicate explicitly what your receivers can fill in on their own. Encourage audience participation. Let your target complete the thought and draw the conclusion. What your target tells themselves will be far more persuasive than anything you say.

A metaphor can be a wonderful way to engage the audience, but a metaphor doesn't work if you explain it. If it requires explanation, get a different metaphor. And actor image doesn't persuade if you spell out the inference you would like the audience to draw. If Danny Trejo tells me to take the anti-sexual assault pledge, I might conclude on my own that I'll feel manly like Danny Trejo if I do likewise. But tell me that I'll feel manly like Danny Trejo and I won't believe it.

As with the previous advice from Sperber and Wilson, leaving everything out that receivers can provide on their own requires clearly understanding how our receivers think. Our message unmistakably communicates how much help we think our audience needs to process it. If we are right, we compliment our audience and suggest an intimacy of connection. If we are wrong, we either insult our audience with too much information or our message is unintelligible because of too little information. The amount of help we offer the audience is critical to our success and understanding how much help to provide requires getting inside the head of the audience.

What we think of our audience is immediately obvious to them. Do we think they are intelligent or unintelligent? Do we think they are well-informed or ill-informed? Do we think they are cool or boring?

Apple's "Think Different" print ads are a good example of employing the art of conversation in persuasion. Many of the ads featured only a portrait of an independent, innovative historical figure along with a small Apple logo and the words "Think Different." At the bottom, in small type, was *www.apple.com*. The historical figures included Alfred Hitchcock, Jim Henson, Maria Callas, Miles Davis, and many others.

The ads deliver on the implicit promise being worth of attention. Each of the figures featured is inherently interesting and we enjoy thinking about how each of them thought differently.

The ads also provide a good example of leaving everything out of the message that receivers can and will provide on their own. The audience fills in the blanks, making the association of Apple products with independent, innovative people who made a difference even though those people may have never used anything by Apple. The ads reveal, undeniably, what Apple thinks of its audience. Apple compliments its audience because it clearly believes its audience will recognize, admire, and seek to emulate these fascinating people. What's left out establishes a degree of complicity between the audience and the brand.

Sometimes, the most powerful part of a persuasive message isn't what we put in, but what we leave out.

Art of Generating Inference

What's left out of a message not only establishes a rapport, it invites participation; it invites inference. In inference, our audience goes beyond the message to draw their own conclusions. When we tell the audience something, the source is automatically suspect. When the audience tells themselves, the source is unimpeachable. People ultimately persuade themselves. The role of our message is to make that possible.

Our persuasive message suggests that the audience behave in a certain way. We may encourage stopping smoking, not experimenting with drugs, making healthier choices in the grocery store, voting for candidate X, or buying brand A. In effect, we are suggesting that the audience join the group of people who have stopped smoking, don't experiment with drugs, make healthier choices in the grocery store, vote for candidate X, or buy brand A.

What evidence does our audience have to evaluate the action we encourage or the group of people we suggest they join?

One critical piece of evidence is the message itself. The audience doesn't just decode the literal meaning of the words used in the message. The audience uses everything about the message—its words, visuals, sound, style, spirit, and the surrounding context—to draw inferences about the action we suggest, the people who act that way, and the sender of the message. Though drawing these inferences may sound like work, it's effortless. It's not only effortless, it's automatic. Just as we automatically form a coherent 3D picture from millions of visual stimuli, the audience members draw these inferences from the message whether they want to or not. The message often has far greater meaning for receivers than the sender intended.

We should think of our persuasive message the way the audience does—as a behavior of the sender that allows the audience to draw inferences. As Fritz Heider, one of the founders of social psychology observed in 1958, "Behavior engulfs the field."[3] What we say is less important than the behavior of our message—that is, how we say it.

Even if we have a logical proposition to communicate, how we attempt to get that point across may say more about who we are than we wish.

In the Super Bowl, Holiday Inn had a logical proposition to get across—if a few thousands of dollars of remodeling can make a person look good, a billion dollars of remodeling should make Holiday Inns look great.

The ad Holiday Inn created to get their point across featured a protagonist at his high school reunion. He meets a former classmate who is a fabulous-looking woman and he attempts to remember the name. While the camera and, apparently, the protagonist leers, the announcer tells us viewers what the enhanced nose, lips, and chest cost in thousands of dollars. At that point, the protagonist comes up with the name. "Bob? Bob Johnson?" he says, dumbstruck. To tie things together, the announcer says that if thousands can make these amazing changes, imagine what a billion can do for Holiday Inn.

But the lizard doesn't stop at the logical proposition. The lizard doesn't even focus on the logical proposition because the message as a whole, not the logical proposition, is the main source of information. The message as a whole tells the audience a lot about what it feels like to stay at a Holiday Inn, about people who stay at Holiday Inn, and about Holiday Inn itself. It seems that experiencing the lovely attractions of a remodeled Holiday Inn is a little like experiencing the lovely attractions of a woman who used to be a male friend. Or, more simply, the message is that a Holiday Inn may be good looking, but may also make you feel a little awkward. Holiday Inn was probably hoping for a different inference.

Albert Mehrabian found that the literal words we use in a message carry only a small portion of the meaning the message communicates. Professor Mehrabian of UCLA explored what makes communications successful in getting across likes and dislikes.[4,5] He found that the words accounted for 7 percent of a message's ability to communicate likes and dislikes, intonation accounted for 38 percent, and facial expressions and body language accounted for 55 percent. The lizard is much more attuned than the conscious mind to the subtleties of the message.

Receivers will pay a lot of attention to everything we do or say and, as we know from the Fundamental Attribution Error, they won't even wonder why we acted or spoke that way. From everything they take in, our audience will draw inferences about the nature of the action we recommend and about the type of people who take that action.

Take advantage of the fact that action implies essence regardless of motivation. Have your candidate publicly act and speak like he or she is the sort of person that voters want and that's how voters will perceive him or her. Voters won't suspect your candidate's motivation. Have your brand act sexy in its advertising and in its packaging, and people will think it's sexy even if it used to be drab. Act as if you are a fashion expert when you are selling shoes and your customers will see you as a fashion expert even if, in reality, you don't care about fashion. You can use action to generate inferences and people are unlikely to suspect what's behind the curtain.

If we explicitly claim that the action we recommend is fun or exciting, or will make you feel masculine or sexy, we are in danger of communicating the opposite. We cannot successfully claim an action is fun. Our message has to be fun. If we wish to associate our brand with fun, we have to juxtapose it with real fun, not just a claim of fun. We have to demonstrate the association. We have to demonstrate the desired quality of the action we recommend in a compelling, memorable way. Only then will the audience believe it and associate that reward with the action.

The audience assumes the timing of the message, the place of the message, the tone of the message, the style of the message, the seriousness of the message, the fun of the message are a reflection of the action we suggest, of the people who act that way, and of the sender. Everything about the message implies what the receiver can expect if they follow our advice.

Budweiser wanted to attract young beer drinkers. Young beer drinkers like to think of themselves as fun and not taking themselves too seriously, and they choose brands that make them look and feel that way. So Budweiser created a commercial that was itself fun and didn't take itself too seriously. The commercial featured frogs who, instead of croaking "ribit," croaked "Bud," "weis," "er." It was a very simple commercial that made no overt claims about Budweiser. But viewers inferred a great deal about Budweiser and its drinkers. Viewers assumed the commercial was a reflection of the brand and the people who drink it.

Even one of the most primitive forms of communication, hand-painted signs, can lead to an inference about a suggested behavior and the people who act that way.

> **Somewhat Irritated**
> **About**
> **Extreme Outrage**

Jon Stewart and Stephen Colbert organized a rally on the Capital Mall in Washington, D.C. They called the event the Rally to Restore Sanity. It was a protest against extremism in any form. The rally suggested calming down, avoiding extremism, and acting reasonably. Hand-painted signs, a staple at any political rally, were much in evidence. A sign can, of course, claim reasonableness and decry extremism, but the sign, "Somewhat irritated about extreme outrage," demonstrated reasonableness in a much more effective way, implying the desirable qualities of the behavior and the people who act that way.

Art of Engagement

An important function of any persuasive message is to gain some attention from the audience. We are subjected daily to roughly 700 ads in traditional media, probably close to that in new media, and many more personal persuasive messages from family, coworkers, bosses, friends, acquaintances, and strangers. We can't give equal time and attention to all those messages. A persuasive message often doesn't need our full attention, but it does benefit from eye movement in its direction as we page through a magazine or newspaper, or standing out a bit from background noise when we participate in a conversation, or momentary hesitation while we surf channels or the Web.

Because our automatic, nonconscious mental system directs us to do what we enjoy, we pay a little more attention to messages we enjoy.

Daniel Berlyne, professor of psychology, University of Toronto, conducted research in experimental aesthetics.[6] He studied how the pleasure of a stimulus varied with its complexity. He found that the pleasure we derive from a stimulus is at its highest when the complexity of the stimulus is at a moderate level. Some complexity enhances pleasure, but if a stimulus is too complex or too simple it gives us less pleasure.

Berlyne's point of view fits with what the intuitive masters of persuasion have been telling us. Some complexity enhances pleasure and improves chances of successful persuasion. Bill Bernbach said that creativity, far from being a self-indulgent art form is "the most practical thing a businessman can employ."[7]

Ancient Greek rhetoricians have studied the most effective way to express an idea and classified the structure of many linguistic techniques as rhetorical figures. McQuarrie and Mick are two marketing professors who analyzed the use of rhetorical figures in advertising and published their results in the *Journal of Consumer Research*. Edward McQuarrie is at the University of California, Santa Clara, and David Glen Mick is at the University of Virginia. According to McQuarrie and Mick, "[W]hen persuasion is the overriding goal, the rhetorical perspective suggests that the manner in which a statement is expressed may be more important than its propositional content."[8] Rhetorical figures are different ways of effectively expressing an idea. A rhetorical figure, also commonly known as a figure of speech, is an artful deviation from what we expect.

A figure of speech adds effectiveness because its deviation from expectation adds a moderate level of complexity. If our message is too simple, it is uninteresting. If our figurative language is too complex, our message is unintelligible. If it is an artful deviation, our figurative language provides what Roland Barthes[9] called "The Pleasure of the Text." Our audience feels "the reward that comes from processing a clever arrangement of signs."[10]

Understandably, figures of speech are pervasive in professional attempts to persuade—that is, in advertising. But any persuasion attempt can benefit from an artful deviation from expectation.

Though there are many different figures of speech, McQuarrie and Mick describe two basic categories: unexpected regularity and unexpected irregularity.

Ordinary speech has a natural variety of sounds. When that natural variety is absent and sounds regularly repeat, we notice. As McQuarrie and Mick point out, examples of this type of unexpected regularity would be chime ("A tradition of trust") and rhyme ("KitchenAid. For the way it's made"). Receivers don't expect words in sequence to begin with the same sound or to rhyme. When they do, it's a slight deviation that draws attention and is a little more enjoyable. The regularity is unexpected.

A second type of unexpected regularity is the reversal of words, phrases, or meanings: "Stops static before static stops you," "Hot prices on cool stuff," and "Easy on eyes. Tough on Tangles."

A message can also be surprisingly irregular. Ordinary speech has logic, grammar, and a syntax that receivers expect. They notice the unexpected irregularity when those rules are violated. Of course, the violation of the rules may render our message unintelligible. That's a risk we take. But our audience believes that our message is one they want to receive, that our message has relevance for them. That is our tacit guarantee. So receivers will try to provide whatever details and context make our message understandable and relevant.

In a message of unexpected irregularity, the receiver looks for and expects to find an underlying meaning. McQuarrie and Mick describe two different classes of unexpected irregularity. The first is substitution.

In substitution, the message is obviously incorrect and the receiver easily provides the correct message.

Hyperbole—that is, exaggeration for the sake of emphasis—is a type of substitution. When iPhone tells us we can browse, download, and stream content at "blazing fast speed," we believe it will be fast, but not really blazing fast. When Sherwin Williams paint tells us that "We Cover the World," we don't take that to be literally true, but we do instantly understand that Sherwin Williams paint can cover just about anything.

Understatement is another form of substitution. In understatement, a message describes something in a way that seems less important, less serious, and less good than it really is. The receiver substitutes the correct message. Volkswagen has long been a master of understatement. In one ad from its recent "Power of German Engineering" campaign, we see two young men talking by the side of the road next to a Volkswagen that has obviously been in a serious accident. Both young men are clearly unhurt. We hear the driver telling his passenger that his dad is going to kill him. As receivers, we quickly supply the correct message: Volkswagen kept them alive.

Destabilization is the second form of unexpected irregularity. Examples of destabilization are pun—"Make fun of the road" (for an automobile), and metaphor—"Say hello to your child's new bodyguard" (for a bandage). Destabilizing statements are statements that may not make literal sense, but do make surprising sense when we think about possible multiple meanings. Sperber and Wilson tell us that people will assume the message makes sense and will work to understand it. The trick is in setting up a puzzle that people enjoy solving. In solving the puzzle of the message, people grasp the deeper meaning.

Many rhetorical figures apply to visual images as well as language. A photo of a baby snuggled up to a bulldog is a powerful visual metaphor for tough but safe.

> **Don't share my wealth.**
> **Share my work ethic.**

At a San Francisco Tea Party rally, one saw rhetorical speech, specifically unexpected regularity, put to good use. "Don't share my wealth. Share my work ethic." Here we see repeated structure and repeated words; simple, noticeable, and memorable.

> **People who**
> **use hyperbole**
> **should be shot.**

Again from the Rally to Restore Sanity comes the sign "People who use hyperbole should be shot." Here we see unexpected irregularity—using hyperbole to criticize hyperbole. It gives the audience credit for its ability to understand and it also provides the audience "the pleasure of the text." It creates the impression that reasonable people are witty not because the message claimed wit, but because the message demonstrated wit.

A little art can help any message be more persuasive. The Ad Council put together a video for LoveHasNoLabels.com. In the video, a large screen in a public space projects the skeletons of couples, families, or friends who are behind the screen. After a minute, each group that had been behind the screen steps out to reveal who they are to the surprise of the crowd. The video promotes tolerance by helping viewers see that, at their essence, people are indistinguishable.

The video leaves out everything that viewers can provide on their own. Viewers' anticipation of and then realization of who is behind the screen is itself the meaning of the video. Viewers tell themselves the message. An announcer never has to belabor the point.

People love to participate in a message. They want to be able to complete a thought or to figure out a simple puzzle. Each couple or group, whose skeletons are projected on the screen, is a simple puzzle for the viewer. Can viewers anticipate the gender, race, age, ability, or disability of the bodies those skeletons inhabit? The video rewards viewers with puzzle after puzzle. The video got 40 million views in its first week on YouTube.

"Don't Mess With Texas"

"Don't mess with Texas" is another illustration of adding a little art to a public service persuasive message. The goal was to reduce littering in Texas. The target members, the people who do most of the littering, are young men. Young Texas men want to feel proud of Texas and, like young men everywhere, they want to appear and to feel tough.

"Don't mess with Texas" shows young men how to get what they want. It's a message they want to receive. "Don't mess with Texas" leaves everything out of the message that young men can provide on their own, creating a bond between the message and the audience. "Don't mess with Texas" acts the way young men want to feel: tough. It doesn't claim toughness; it demonstrates toughness and, in doing so, effectively associates the act of not littering with the feeling of toughness. The message also reveals that the sender thinks the audience appreciates toughness. Finally, "Don't mess with Texas" uses figurative language with unexpected irregularity, specifically a pun on "mess," to make the message a little more interesting and memorable.

Of course, the campaign included many other elements, like tough members of the Dallas Cowboys as spokespersons. But with or without the Dallas Cowboys, "Don't mess with Texas" is powerfully persuasive communication.

Whatever you say to persuade, say it a little unexpectedly. We have learned the value of engaging the automatic mind in persuasion attempts. The automatic mind enjoys finding the meaning within a clever message. We have learned that the ancient rhetoricians were right—what you say is less important than how you say it. People will infer qualities of the option you recommend and infer qualities of the people who take that option from how you say what you say. A boring message leads receivers to infer an uninteresting option and uninteresting people who take it. A fun message leads receivers to infer a fun option and fun people who take it.

Rhetoricians have shown us how to be a little more interesting, surprising, and engaging in what we say—figures of speech, minor deviations from expected expression that trigger the receiver's attention, and participation in a message. Linguists have classified figures of speech in lists that distinguish from 45 to 250 different types. You might check them out for inspiration.

Your clever message compliments your target. They automatically understand that you believe they will get it and enjoy it. A complimented audience is more likely to comply.

Even if you are just talking to your kids, a slightly unexpected request is more likely to be followed and remembered.

Crafting a persuasive message may seem a difficult assignment. Whole industries with legions of professionals struggle with the task. However, all persuasion can apply a little of the art of conversation, a little of the art of generating inference, and a little of the art of engagement. When it does, it stands a better chance of changing the way its target acts.

10

PERSONAL PERSUASION

The secrets of persuasion described in the previous chapters apply to persuasion in all its forms. The secrets are grounded in the nature of the human mind, so as long as the target of persuasion is one or more humans, all seven secrets are useful.

There are three forms of persuasion:

1. Macro-occupational—attempting to change the behavior of millions of people at the same time (for example, marketing Cheerios or attracting shoppers to Target).

2. Micro-occupational—attempting to change the behavior of many people, one or a few people at a time (for example, selling cars in a showroom or canvassing for votes).

3. Micro-personal—attempting to change the behavior of one individual we already know well (for example, encouraging a child to stay in school).

All three forms can take advantage of the seven secrets of persuasion because the lizard inside controls behavior in all three cases.

However, the forms differ in target, tools, intimacy, and importance of the individual interaction.

When we engage in macro persuasion (marketing Cheerios for example), the job is to change the behavior of many people, millions. The target is mass. The tools of macro persuasion are of course things that can simultaneously affect many people's behavior: price, packaging, distribution, Website, hours of operation, location, and advertising and public relations in any manifestation. The interactions are far from intimate. We don't personally know the individuals in our target and we don't come into contact during the interaction. In macro persuasion we have many, often millions of chances to succeed. A success rate of 20 percent in macro persuasion would make us heroes. If we could get 20 percent of the people who were going to buy Corn Flakes to buy Cheerios instead, we would be the toast of the business world. If we could, through macro persuasion, get 20 percent of the people who were going to vote for the other candidate to vote for our candidate, we are unlikely to ever lose another election. If we could, through macro persuasion, get 20 percent of the kids who were not exercising to begin to exercise vigorously, we would have a dramatic impact on the problem of childhood obesity. Because a 20 percent success rate is spectacular, each individual target interaction is less critical. Though we may fail with one, we have many more chances to succeed.

Macro persuasion is always occupational. It's a job. It may be something we do for money, like marketing Cheerios, encouraging shoppers to visit Target, or encouraging people to use mass transportation. It may be something we do "pro bono," like helping the American Cancer Society solicit contributions. But macro persuasion is a job. It is a task for which we have responsibility and feel obligation.

Micro persuasion can be either occupational or personal.

If I am a salesperson in an automobile dealership, a salesperson in a shoe store, an insurance agent, or a door-to-door canvasser for a political candidate, I engage in micro-occupational persuasion. My job is to change the behavior of many people, but surely not millions. I encounter these people *one or a few at a time*. Many elements of my interaction with the target are predetermined and outside my control, such as price, packaging, distribution, and hours. My primary tool is myself—my appearance, my facial expressions, my body language, my enthusiasm, how I appear to feel about the person I meet, and my ability to deal with the lizard inside the person I am interacting with. Can I, by the way I act, improve the association of the car with excitement, the association of the shoes with style, the association of the life insurance with caring responsibility, or the association of my candidate with prosperity? Can I show the customer how to get something he or she wants or how to feel the way he or she wants to feel by taking a test drive, by buying a particular type of shoe, by insuring against accidental death, or by voting for my candidate? Can I change the experience of driving that car, of wearing those shoes, of having that insurance, of voting for that candidate by changing that person's expectation? Can everything I say be about what the target wants? Can I make everything I say something that person will be happy to hear?

As a salesperson, insurance agent, or door-to-door canvasser, in other words, as someone engaged in micro-occupational persuasion, my interaction with the target is one-to-one, or one-to-few. The target and I meet. We are in direct contact for the duration of that interaction even though we may never see each other again. Micro-occupational persuasion is far more intimate than macro persuasion, but not nearly as intimate as personal persuasion. Each interaction in micro-occupational persuasion is much more important than a macro persuasion interaction because I don't have millions of chances to succeed. When I fail to persuade one person in micro-occupational persuasion, another one will come along, but the supply is not unlimited.

Many commercial, public service, or political marketing campaigns involve both macro and micro persuasion. Macro persuasion draws people into the showroom. Micro persuasion by the salesperson on the floor closes the deal. Macro persuasion gets parents to ask their medical professional about vaccinations. The medical professional completes the persuasion and schedules the shots. Macro persuasion gets people to lean toward one candidate. The canvasser guides people to vote early.

Personal Persuasion

Personal persuasion is quite different. The target in personal persuasion is not millions of people, nor is it many people one at a time. In personal persuasion, the target is an individual whom we already know well. The target might be a spouse we would like to stop smoking, a child we want to stay in school, a neighbor whose dog is keeping us awake at night, a boss we are hoping will give us a raise, or an older parent who we are encouraging to sell the family home. The persuasion interaction is intimate. We are not only face-to-face during the interaction; we have an ongoing, close relationship before and after the persuasion attempt. Each persuasion attempt is crucial. Success is all or nothing. If the persuasion attempt fails, there's no one else. Our persuasion rate is either 100 percent or it is zero.

Whenever we personally attempt to get an individual we already know to change their behavior, the situation is potentially confrontational and volatile. An attempt at personal persuasion unmistakably tells the target that we disapprove of their current behavior. Any persuasion attempt will likely be perceived as a criticism, putting the target on the defensive.

Because of the importance and the difficulty of an attempt at personal persuasion, the secrets of persuasion are even more important. The lizard inside is still in charge and we need every edge we can get.

Personal persuasion can make use of all seven secrets of persuasion but, to avoid confrontation, we might begin with an emphasis on two: (1) aiming at the act rather than the attitude and (2) fulfilling desires rather than changing desires.

Aiming at the Act Rather than the Attitude

Aiming to change an individual's attitude calls forth intellectual antibodies and those antibodies are made all the more powerful and emotional by the implied disapproval of the target's current attitude.

If it's possible to adjust the situation so the desired behavior becomes a more natural, a more expected, an easier option, or the only option, we might change the target's behavior without confronting their attitude.

If we are concerned about a spouse drinking and driving, we can make sure we get to the event by cab or by public transportation. Drinking and driving is no longer an option. We will still get the outcome we want, but the process is a lot less painful. And, as we know, the target's behavior change is quite likely to lead to attitudinal change without any further intervention on our part.

For many people, back-seat driving (which usually occurs from the front passenger seat) is irresistible. The back-seat driver is rolling around at a high rate of speed surrounded by others doing likewise. No matter how much confidence a back-seat driver has in the actual driver, the urge for a sense of control is natural and powerful. The foot pressing the floor mat, the hand pushing on the dashboard, and the sudden intake of breadth all ask the driver to drive differently. And the back-seat driver cannot refrain from making helpful comments about speed and spacing. Nothing the driver says will change the behavior. Even if the back-seat driver wants to behave differently, he or she can't. Being a back-seat driver is not a choice, it arises from an overpowering urge for self-preservation. Any attempt to change the behavior by information, reasoning, or complaint will have little impact other than to offend the back-seat driver. But the actual driver or the back-seat driver can adjust the situation and painlessly change the behavior. Distraction is all that is required. If the back-seat driver is busy on a computer tablet, for example, surfing the Web, answering e-mail, or playing solitaire, the behavior ceases.

Without ever appearing to criticize eating habits, you can fill up your spouse with healthy food and thereby lessen his or her consumption of junk food.

Without complaint, you can reduce urination "spillage" on the part of boys of all ages by changing the circumstances. Try placing a fly decal at the proper spot in the toilet bowl. Airports have found that such a target improves aim and reduces "spillage" by as much as 80 percent.[1]

Often, the easiest way to change behavior is to change circumstances. Different circumstances call forth different behavior.

Fulfilling Desires Rather Than Changing Desires

Persuasion in general, and personal persuasion in particular, can't be about what I, the persuader, want. The only way to persuade anyone of anything is to talk about what they want and show them how to get it. Personal persuasion doesn't involve talking to the target about doing what I want them to do. It is about helping the target find a better way to get something they already want. Persuasion is about fulfilling desires, not changing them. Personal persuasion requires understanding what the target wants and finding a connection between something they want and the behavior I would like to encourage. If I'm not thinking about and talking about what the target wants, my chances of success in persuasion are almost nil.

When we offer adolescent boys the opportunity to benefit financially from energy savings, we not only change the situation, we give ourselves the chance to talk about what the boys want and show them how to get it. We don't have to change their desires. We can help them fulfill their desires. We no longer have to lecture them about energy costs and we don't have to hound them about the temperature in their room. Their behavior will change because a change in behavior helps them get what they want.

If the person feels that by changing behavior he or she is bending to my will, I have little chance of success. When I change the situation or when I am able to show the target how to get what they want—fulfilling desires rather than changing desires—I defuse the drama. If the target feels the revised behavior is a response to a new situation or a way to get what he or she desires, the target is persuading themselves.

Personal persuasion is difficult and we will live with the success or failure day in and day out for a long time. Begin by defusing the drama, but don't stop there. Unearth the reward that might motivate a change in behavior. Focus on what it will feel like to take your recommended option. Enhance the person's experience by improving their expectation. And tell the target something they would like to hear.

Through it all, employ the language of the lizard. The lizard is as powerful in the person we know as it is in the person we don't. Because we know the person well, we are tempted to ignore the lizard. We imagine, with our inside knowledge of the target, we can persuade by the power of our arguments. We can't.

The lizard doesn't yield to reasoned arguments, no matter how well-crafted.

CONCLUSION

The secrets of persuasion are effective because they address the lizard inside: our automatic, nonconscious mental system. We know now this automatic system affects all our choices and is the sole influence in many. But we learned this only recently.

In the past, the theory of persuasion had focused on the us we are familiar with: the reflective mental system, the only mental system available to consciousness. The theory emphasized factual information, reasoning, and an orderly flow from information to attitude to behavior.

However, successful practitioners of persuasion—from the ancient rhetoricians, to modern, expert salespeople like Dale Carnegie and Bill Bernbach—didn't let the theory of persuasion stop them from doing what they knew worked. They intuitively spoke to the automatic, nonconscious mental system.

To be successful, you need to deal with the lizard inside. The lizard is much faster than our reflective mental system, has much greater capacity, works effortlessly, can't be turned off, is focused on the here and now, and is capable of performing tasks that are either innate (like seeing) or learned through great repetition (like speaking English).

In order to persuade the lizard, the automatic, nonconscious mental system, speak its language:

- Mental availability. Your automatic system pays the most attention to and assumes the importance of things and people that come most easily to mind.

- Association. An idea in the mind activates other associated ideas and each of these ideas activates still more ideas. Associations occur even if you don't want them to. You can't stop association, but you can adjust it.

- Action. For the lizard, you are what you do no matter why you do it.

- Emotion .The automatic system uses emotion to communicate its desires and is swayed by emotion—liking, repulsion, fear, or happiness.

- The preferences and behavior of others. The automatic, nonconscious mental system uses the preferences and behavior of others to help form its own preferences and even to help evaluate how happy it is with a choice it has already made.

Aim at what people do, not their attitude. Many actions are spontaneous and don't pass through an attitudinal screen.

Changing the act is your ultimate goal. Aim at that goal. Fortunately, the act may be easier to change than the attitude. And changing the act is likely to be a more effective way of changing the attitude than the reverse. When you aim to change the act, you have a much wider array of persuasive tools to work with. Lay out the leaky hose—the series of smaller action steps that lead to the ultimate act you aim to encourage or discourage. Figure out precisely where to focus your persuasive attempt to have the biggest impact on the outcome.

Talk about what the target wants even if the target members don't consciously know exactly what they want. When you stop trying to change what people want and instead try to show people how to get what they want, your message becomes dramatically different. Your persuasive attempts become less strident, preachy, and moralistic and more focused on the desires of the target. Only then will the target listen.

Remember: With many daily decisions, the automatic system, not the reflective system, is in charge and factual information is not the answer. Rational information can have little impact on a decision that is not rationally made.

When identifying the desires that can motivate the action you wish, remember:

- Don't think small. Offer to fulfill a fundamental human desire. Other desires have less magic.

- Look for a universal motivation. Similarities in motivation across groups will generally be greater than differences.

- Offer a reward that is immediate, certain, and emotional.

Don't ask people why they do what they do, or how they choose, or what's most important in their decision. People don't know the answer, but they think they do. Bad information is worse than no information.

Unearth the answer with some basic research, whether informal or formal. See what people who already act as you would like associate with that action. Decide whether the same association would also motivate your target. If so, begin to build the association. If not, find something else in the overlap of what your target wants and the possible outcomes of the action. Build that association.

Focus on feelings. When you focus on a feeling rather than an attribute, you:

- Gain the power of promising an end rather than a means.

- Gain precision because, without guidance, an attribute can lead to many different feelings.

- Turn a delayed, uncertain, rational benefit into an immediate, certain, and emotional reward.

- Tap into an additional class of rewards that doesn't depend on the physical experience of the action you recommend—actor image rewards.

When you promise the feeling of participating in an attractive actor image, you:

- Offer your target the opportunity to appear to others as the person they would like to be—public image enhancement.

- Offer your target the opportunity to appear to themselves as the person they would like to be—self-image enhancement.

- Imply a variety of positive qualities of the action naturally associated with that actor image.

Perception is an unconscious process carried out by the lizard inside, the automatic mental system. Expectation guides perception. You can change the experience by changing the expectation. If we expect carrots to taste a little better, they will.

What we see, feel, taste, or smell depends to a great degree on what we expect to see, feel, taste, or smell. What the eye sees depends, only in part, on what is there to be seen. What the eye sees also depends on what it expects to see. No eye is without expectation. No eye is innocent. You can create the expectation.

Communication may not be the best way to change the behavior of the target. Changing the situation will often be more effective in getting the target to act differently.

When you do use communication to persuade, remember that what you literally say may be less important than how you say it.

The lizard responds to art.

All persuasion can use a little of the art of conversation—making a tacit guarantee that the message is one the audience will want to receive and literally communicating only what the audience cannot provide on their own, establishing a degree of complicity and a level of emotional closeness.

All persuasion can use a little of the art of generating inference—thinking of the message not so much as content, but more as the behavior of people who act the way you would like the audience to act because behavior implies much more about those people than you could say.

And all persuasion can use a little of the art of engagement—making your message unexpected, encouraging the audience to seek the pleasure that comes from deciphering a clever arrangement of signs.

With a little art you increase your chance of persuasion.

Persuasion is defined as convincing by means of reasoned argument. The definition is wrong.

Because the remarkably capable lizard is in charge of most decisions, reasoned argument is a waste of time. You can only persuade the lizard if you speak its language and show the lizard a better way to fulfill its desires.

CHAPTER NOTES

1. Getting to Know the Lizard

1. Richard Thaler and Cass Sunstein, *Nudge: Improving Decisions About Health, Wealth, and Happiness* (New York: Penguin, 2008), 28.

2. Jonathan Miller, "Going Unconscious," *The New York Review of Books*, April 20, 1995, 59-65.

3. David Eagleman, *Incognito: the Secret Lives of the Brain* (New York: Pantheon Books, a division of Random House, Inc., 2011), 9-12.

4. Daniel Kahneman, *Thinking Fast and Think Slow* (New York: Farrar, Straus and Giroux, 2011), 19-30.

5. Thaler and Sunstein, *Nudge: Improving Decisions About Health, Wealth, and Happiness,* 19-20.

6. Eagleman, *Incognito: the Secret Lives of the Brain,* 4.

7. The chart owes a lot to Timothy D. Wilson, *Strangers to Ourselves* (Cambridge, Massachusetts: The Belknap Press of Harvard University Press, 2002) and Thaler and Sunstein, *Nudge: Improving Decisions About Health, Wealth, and Happiness.*

8. Wen Li, et al., "Neural and Behavioral Evidence for Affective Priming from Unconsciously Perceived Emotional Facial Expressions and the Influence of Trait Anxiety," *Journal of Cognitive Neuroscience* 20:1 (2008): 95-107.

9. Will Rogers, *Saturday Evening Post*, November 6, 1926, 231. Rogers specifically spelled "dident."

10. Tor Norretranders, *The User Illusion* (New York: Viking, 1991), 124-156.

11. Pawel Lewicki, Thomas Hill, and Elizabeth Bizot, "Acquisition of Procedural Knowledge about a Pattern of Stimuli that Cannot Be Articulated," *Cognitive Psychology* 20 (1988): 24-37.

12. Antoine Bechara, et al., "Deciding Advantageously Before Knowing the Advantageous Strategy," *Science* 235 (28 February, 1997): 1293-1295.

13. James Crimmins and Chris Callahan, "Reducing Road Rage: The Role of Target Insight in Advertising for Social Change," *Journal of Advertising Research* 43(4) (2003): 381-389.

14. Amos Tversky and Daniel Kahneman, "Rational Choice and the Framing of Decisions," *The Journal of Business* Vol. 59, No. 4, Part 2: *The Behavioral Foundations of Economic Theory* (1986): S251-S278.

2. Speak the Language of the Lizard: Basic Grammar

1. Daniel Kahneman and Amos Tversky, "Judgment under Uncertainty: Heuristics and Biases," *Science* 185 (September,1974): 1124-1131.

2. Wayne D. Hoyer and Steven P. Brown, "Effects of Brand Awareness on Choice for a Common, Repeat-Purchase

Product," *Journal of Consumer Research* 17, No. 2 (Sep., 1990): 141-148.

3. Scott Plous, *The Psychology of Judgment and Decision Making* (New York: McGraw-Hill, Inc., 1993), 121.

4. Ibid, 78-80.

5. Thaler and Sunstein, *Nudge: Improving Decisions About Health, Wealth, and Happiness*, 23.

6. John A. Bargh, Mark Chen, and Lara Burrows, "Automaticity of Social Behavior: Direct Effects of Trait Construct and Stereotype Activation on Action," *Journal of Personality and Social Psychology* 71 (1996): 230-244.

7. Robert B. Zajonc, "Attitudinal Effects of Mere Exposure," *Journal of Personality and Social Psychology* 9, No. 2, Part 2 (1968): 1-27.

8. Kahneman, *Thinking Fast and Think Slow*, 62.

9. Brian Wansink, Andrew S. Hanks, and Kirsikka Kalpainen, "Slim by Design: Kitchen Counter Correlates of Obesity," *Health Education and Behavior,* (October 19, 2015): 1-7. Of course, what's visible in the kitchen and one's weight are mutually causal. People who are overweight tend to have junk food out in their kitchen, and people who have junk food out in their kitchen tend to eat it and are overweight. Similarly, people who are careful what they eat tend to have fruit out and people who have fruit out tend to eat more fruit and less junk food and are thinner.

10. Kahneman, *Thinking Fast and Think Slow*, 52.

11. Christopher Helman, "David Crane's Green Vision For Carbon-Belching NRG Energy," *Forbes*, July 21, 2014, 1-2.

3. Speak the Language of the Lizard: Style

1. Plous, *The Psychology of Judgment and Decision Making*, 180-181.

2. Fritz Heider, *The Psychology of Interpersonal Relations* (New York: Wiley, 1958), 54.

3. Mark Twain, *The Adventures of Tom Sawyer* (Page By Page Books, 1876), Chapter II, p. 1.

4. Robert B. Cialdini, PhD, *Influence: The Psychology of Persuasion* (New York: Harper Collins Publishers, 1984), 17.

5. Paul Slovic, et al., "The Affect Heuristic" In *Heuristics and Biases: The Psychology of Intuitive Judgment* ed. Thomas Gilovitch and Daniel Kahneman (New York: Cambridge University Press, 2002), 397-420.

6. Jonathan Haidt, "The Emotional Dog and Its Rational Tail: A Social Intuitionist Approach to Moral Judgment," *Psychological Review* 108, (2001): 814-838.

7. Kahneman, *Thinking Fast and Think Slow*, 201.

8. Matt Ridley, *The Red Queen: Sex and the Evolution of Human Nature* (Great Britain: Penguin Books Ltd., 1993), 146.

9. Andrew Pomiankowski, "How to Find the Top Male," *Nature* 347 (1990): 616-617.

10. Andrew Ehrenberg, Gerald J. Goodhardt, and T. Patrick Barwise, "Double Jeopardy Revisited," *Journal of Marketing,* 54 (July, 1990): 82-91.

11. Harriet Barovick, "What's So Funny? Laughter-Yoga Fans Hail the Benefits of Giggling for No Reason," *Time*, September 13, 2010, http://content.time.com/time/magazine/article/0,9171,2015766,00.html.

12. Ap Dijksterhuis and John A. Bargh, "The Perception-Behavior Expressway: Automatic Effects of Social Perception on Social Behavior," *Advances in Experimental Social Psychology* 33 (2001): 1-40.

13. Sushil Bikhchandani, David Hirshleifer, and Ivo Welch, "Learning from the Behavior of Others: Conformity, Fads, and Informational Cascades," *Journal of Economic Perspectives* 12, Number 3 (Summer, 1998): 151-170.

14. Matthew J. Salgonic, Peter Sheridan Dodds, and Duncan J. Watts, "Experimental Study of Inequality and Unpredictability in an Artificial Cultural Market," *Science* 311 (2006): 854-856.

15. Cialdini, *Influence: The Psychology of Persuasion,* 237-271.

16. Brian Elbel, et al., "Calorie Labeling And Food Choices: A First Look At The Effects On Low-Income People In New York City," *Health Affairs* 28(6) (2009): 1110-1121.

17. Thomas E. Barry and Daniel J. Howard, "A Review and Critique of Hierarchy of Effects in Advertising," *International Journal of Advertising* 9, 2 (1990): 121-135.

18. Benjamin Libet, "Unconscious Cerebral Initiative and the Role of Conscious Will in Voluntary Action," *Behavioral and Brain Sciences* 8 (1985): 529-566.

19. Chun Siong Soon, et al., "Unconscious Determinants of Free Decisions in the Human Brain," *Nature Neuroscience* 11(5) (April 13, 2008): 543-545.

20. Timothy D. Wilson, *Strangers to Ourselves* (Cambridge, Massachusetts: The Belknap Press of Harvard University Press, 2002), 47.

4. Aim at the Act, Not the Attitude

1. Timothy C. Brock and Melanie C. Green, *Persuasion: Psychological Insights and Perspectives* (Thousand Oaks: Sage Publications, 2005), 3.

2. Johann Wolfgang Von Goethe (1749-1832), German poet, novelist, and dramatist, n.d.

3. Icek Ajzen and Martin Fishbein, "Influence of Attitudes on Behavior," In *The Handbook of Attitudes*, ed. Dolores Albarracín, Blair T. Johnson, and Mark P. Zanna (Mahwah, NJ: Lawrence Earlbaum Associates, 2005), 173-221.

4. Allan W. Wicker, "Attitudes versus Actions: The Relationship of Verbal and Overt Behavioral Responses to Attitude Objects," *Journal of Social Issues* XXV, Number 4 (1969): 41-78.

5. S.M. Corey, "Professed Attitudes and Actual Behavior," *Journal of Educational Psychology* 28(4) (1937): 271-280.

6. Ajzen and Fishbein, "Influence of Attitudes on Behavior," 173-221.

7. "Throwing Out the Free Market Playbook: An Interview with Naomi Klein," *Solutions* 3, 1 (February, 2012), http://www.thesolutionsjournal.com/node/1053.

8. Joshua Klayman and Young-Wan Ha, "Confirmation, Disconfirmation, and Information in Hypothesis Testing," *Psychological Review* XCIV (1987): 221-228.

9. Plous, *The Psychology of Judgment and Decision Making*, 180-181.

10. William James, *William James: Writings 1878-1899* (Cambridge, MA: Harvard University Press, 1984), 751.

11. David T. Neal, Wendy Wood, and Jeffrey M. Quinn, "Habits—A Repeat Performance," *Current Directions in Psychological Science* 15, No. 4 (2006): 198-202.

12. Thaler and Sunstein, *Nudge: Improving Decisions About Health, Wealth, and Happiness.*

13. Joel Cooper, Robert Mirabile, and Steven J. Scher, "Actions and Attitudes: The Theory of Cognitive Dissonance," In *Persuasion: Psychological Insights and Perspectives*, ed. Timothy C. Green and Melanie C. Brock (Thousand Oaks, CA: Sage Publications, 2005), 66.

14. Leon Festinger and James M. Carlsmith, "Cognitive Consequences of Forced Compliance," *Journal of Abnormal and Social Psychology* 58(2) (1959): 203-210.

15. Michael R. Leippe and Donna Eisenstadt, "Generalization of Dissonance Reduction: Decreasing Prejudice through Induced Compliance," *Journal of Personality and Social Psychology* 67 (1994): 395-413.

16. Philip G. Zimbardo, et al., "Communicator Effectiveness in Producing Public Conformity and Private Attitude Change," *Journal of Personality* 33 (1965): 233-255.

17. Jack W. Brehm, "Post Decision Changes in Desirability of Alternatives," *Social Psychology* 52 (1956): 384-389.

18. Daryl J. Bem, "Self-Perception: An Alternative Interpretation of Cognitive Dissonance Phenomena," *Psychological Review* 74 (1967): 183-200.

19. Joseph P. Allen, et al., "Preventing Teen Pregnancy and Academic Failure: Experimental Evaluation of a Developmentally Based Approach," *Child Development* 64 (1997): 729-742.

20. Elisabetta Gentile and Scott A. Imberman, "Dressed for Success? The Effect of School Uniforms on

Student Achievement and Behavior," *Journal of Urban Economics* 71(1) (2012): 1-17.

21. Dana R. Carney, Amy J.C. Cuddy, and Andy J. Yap, "Power Posing: Brief Nonverbal Displays Affect Neuroendocrine Levels and Risk Tolerance," *Psychological Science* 21 (10) (2010): 1363-1368.

22. Kurt Vonnegut, *Mother Night* (1961), BrainyQuote.com, Xplore Inc., 2016. http://www.brainyquote.com/quotes/quotes/k/kurtvonneg124385.html, accessed June 8, 2016.

23. Baruch Fischhoff and Ruth Beyth, "'I Knew it Would Happen': Remembered Probabilities of Once—Future Things," *Organizational Behavior and Human Performance* 13 (1975): 1-16.

24. Cialdini, *Influence: The Psychology of Persuasion,* 71-74.

25. Steven J. Sherman, "On the Self-Erasing Nature of Errors of Prediction," *Journal of Personality and Social Psychology* 39 (1980): 211-221.

26. Jonathan L. Freedman and Scott C. Fraser, "Compliance Without Pressure: The Foot-In-The-Door Technique," *Journal of Personality and Social Psychology* 4, No. 2 (1966): 195-202.

5. Don't Change Desires, Fulfill Them

1. Dale Carnegie, *How to Win Friends and Influence People* (New York: Simon and Schuster, 1936), 24.

2. Dena M. Gromet, Howard Kunreuther, Richard P. Larrick, "Political Ideology Affects Energy-Efficiency Attitudes and Choices," *Proceedings of the National Academy of Sciences USA* 110 (2013): 9314–9319.

3. A.H. Maslow, "A Theory of Human Motivation," *Psychological Review* 50 (1943): 370-396.

4. Donald E. Brown, *Human Universals* (New York: McGraw-Hill, Inc., 1991), 130-141.

5. John G. Lynch Jr. and Gal Zauberman, "When Do You Want It? Time, Decisions, and Public Policy," *Journal of Public Policy and Marketing* 25 (1) (Spring, 2006): 67-78.

6. Ted O'Donoghue and Matthew Rabin, "Doing It Now or Later," *The American Economic Review* 89 No. 1 (March, 1999): 103-124.

7. Amos Tversky and Daniel Kahneman, "Rational Choice and the Framing of Decisions," *The Journal of Business* 59, No. 4, Part 2: *The Behavioral Foundations of Economic Theory,* (1986): S251-S278.

8. "Expected value" is the sum of the probability of each possible outcome multiplied by its value. For Option 2, the expected value is (.8) ($45) + (.2) ($0) = $36.

9. Plous, *The Psychology of Judgment and Decision Making,* 99-100.

10. Recently, Miller Brewing has brought back the phrase "Miller Time," but is now using it in reference to its light beer, Miller Lite.

6. Never Ask, Unearth

1. Bill Bernbach, *Bill Bernbach Said,* http://www.ddb.com/pdf/bernbach.pdf, n.d.

2. Wilson, *Strangers to Ourselves,* 97.

3. Michael S. Gazzaniga, "Right Hemisphere Language Following Brain Bisection: a 20 Year Perspective," *American Psychologist* 38, No. 5 (May, 1983): 525-537.

4. Eagleman, *Incognito: the Secret Lives of the Brain,* 133.

5. Richard E. Nisbett and Timothy DeCamp Wilson, "Telling More Than We Can Know: Verbal Reports on Mental Processes," *Psychological Review* 84 (1977): 231-259.

6. Wilson, *Strangers to Ourselves*, 101.

7. Kahneman, *Thinking Fast and Think Slow*, 153.

8. Pew Research Center Report, "Campaign 2016: Modest Interest, High Stakes," http://www.people-press.org/2015/04/02/campaign-2016-modest-interest-high-stakes/.

9. Fox News Poll, "Shakeup in GOP field after first debate, Sanders gains on Clinton," http://www.foxnews.com/politics/2015/08/16/fox-news-poll-shakeup-in-gop-field-after-first-debate-sanders-gains-on-clinton.html.

10. Joseph Hair, et al., *Essentials of Marketing Research* (Toronto, ON: McGraw-Hill, 2008), Deli Depot data set. Analysis by author.

11. Rogers and Hammerstein, lyrics to "Some Enchanted Evening," *South Pacific*, www.lyricsmode.com/lyrics/r/rodgers_and_hammerstein/some_enchanted_evening.html.

7. Focus on Feeling

1. Antonio Damasio, *The Feeling of What Happens: Body and Emotion in the Making of Consciousness* (New York: Harcourt Brace. 1999), 41.

2. Bechara, et al., "Deciding Advantageously Before Knowing the Advantageous Strategy," 1293-1295.

3. George Loewenstein, "Out of Control: Visceral Influences on Behavior," *Organizational Behavior and*

Human Decision Processes 65, No. 3 (March, 1996): 272-292.

4. Thomas Gilovich, Kenneth Savitsky, and Victoria Husted Medvec, "The Spotlight Effect in Social Judgment: An Egocentric Bias in Estimates of the Salience of One's Own Actions and Appearance," *Journal of Personality and Social Psychology* 78, No. 2 (2000): 211-221.

8. Create Experience With Expectation

1. E.H. Gombrich, *Art and Illusion: a Study in the Psychology of Pictorial Representation* (Princeton, N.J.: Princeton University Press, 1960).

2. Thomas N. Robinson, et al., "Effects of Fast Food Branding on Young Children's Taste Preferences," *Archives of Pediatric Adolescent Medicine* 161(8) (2007): 792-797.

3. Samuel M. McClure, et al., "Neural Correlates of Behavioral Preference for Culturally Familiar Drinks," *Neuron* 44 (October 14, 2004): 379-387.

4. Leonard Lee, Shane Frederick, and Dan Ariely, "Try It, You'll Like It: The Influence of Expectation, Consumption, and Revelation on Preferences for Beer," *Association for Psychological Science* 17, No. 12 (2006): 1054-1058.

5. James C. Makens, "Effect of Brand Preference upon Consumers' Perceived Taste of Turkey Meat," *Journal of Applied Psychology* 49 (1965): 261-263.

6. Jeffrey S. Nevid, "Effects of Brand Labeling on Ratings of Product Quality," *Perceptual and Motor Skills* 53 (1981): 407-410.

7. Ralph I. Allison and Kenneth P. Uhl, "Influence of Beer Brand Identification on Taste Perception," *Journal of Marketing Research* 1 (1964): 36-39.

8. Brian Wansink, Sea Bum Park, Steven Sonka, and Michelle Morganosky, "How Soy Labeling Influences Preference and Taste," *International Food and Agribusiness Management Review* 3 (2000): 85-94.

9. Jerry C. Olson and Philip A. Dover, "Cognitive Effects of Deceptive Advertising," *Journal of Marketing Research* 15 (1978): 29-38.

10. Jane Wardle and Wendy Solomons, "Naughty but Nice: A Laboratory Study of Health Information and Food Preferences in a Community Sample," *Health Psychology* 13 (1994): 180-183.

11. Deborah J. Bowen, et al., "Effects of Expectancies and Personalized Feedback on Fat Consumption, Taste, and Preference," *Journal of Applied Social Psychology* 22 (1992): 1061-1079.

12. Paul Slovic, et al., "The Affect Heuristic" in *Heuristics and Biases: The Psychology of Intuitive Judgment,* ed. Thomas Gilovitch and Daniel Kahneman, 397-420.

13. Stephen J. Hoch and Young-Won Ha, "Consumer Learning: Advertising and the Ambiguity of Product Experience," *Journal of Consumer Research* 13, No. 2 (1986): 221-233.

14. Zajonc, "Attitudinal Effects of Mere Exposure," 1-27.

15. Wayne D. Hoyer and Steven P. Brown, "Effects of Brand Awareness on Choice for a Common, Repeat-Purchase Product," *Journal of Consumer Research* 17, No. 2 (Sep., 1990): 141-148.

16. John Deighton, "The Interaction of Advertising and Evidence," *Journal of Consumer Research* 11 (December, 1984): 763-770.

17. Hoch and Ha, "Consumer Learning: Advertising and the Ambiguity of Product Experience," 221-233.

18. Stacy Flaherty and Mimi Minnick, *Marlboro Oral History and Documentation Project, ca. 1926-1986*, http://americanhistory.si.edu/archives/d7198.htm, Smithsonian Institution, 2000.

9. Add a Little Art

1. Dan Sperber and Deirdre Wilson, *Relevance: Communication and Cognition, 2nd ed.* (Oxford: Blackwell Publishers Ltd, 1995), 31-38.

2. Richard E. Grandy and Richard Warner, "Paul Grice" in *Stanford Encyclopedia of Philosophy*, edited by Edward N. Zalta (Stanford CA: The Metaphysics Research Lab, Center for the Study of Language and Information, Stanford University, 2009).

3. Heider, *The Psychology of Interpersonal Relations*, 54.

4. Albert Mehrabian and Morton Wiener, "Decoding of Inconsistent Communications," *Journal of Personality and Social Psychology* 6 (1) (1967): 109-114.

5. Albert Mehrabian and Susan R. Ferris, "Inference of Attitudes from Nonverbal Communication in Two Channels," *Journal of Consulting Psychology* 31(3) (June, 1967): 248-552.

6. D.E. Berlyne, "A Theory of Human Curiosity," *British Journal of Psychology*, 45:3 (1954): 180-191.

7. Bill Bernbach, *Bill Bernbach Said*, http://www.ddb.com/pdf/bernbach.pdf, n.d.

8. Edward F. McQuarrie and David Glen Mick, "Figures of Rhetoric in Advertising Language," *Journal of Consumer Research* 22, No. 4 (1996): 424-438.

9. Roland Barthes, *The Pleasure of the Text* (New York: Hill and Wang, 1975).

10. McQuarrie and Mick, "Figures of Rhetoric in Advertising Language," 424-438.

10. Personal Persuasion

1. Richard H. Thaler and Cass R. Sunstein, "Easy Does It," *The New Republic*, April 8, 2008, https://newrepublic.com/article/63355/easy-does-it.

BIBLIOGRAPHY

Ajzen, Icek, and Martin Fishbein. "Influence of Attitudes on Behavior." In *The Handbook of Attitudes,* by Dolores Albarracin, Blair T. Johnson, Mark P. Zanna, 173-221. Mahwah, NJ: Lawrence Earlbaum Associates, 2005.

Allen, Joseph P., Susan Philliber, Scott Herrling, and Gabriel P. Kuperminc. "Preventing Teen Pregnancy and Academic Failure: Experimental Evaluation of a Developmentally Based Approach." *Child Development* 64 (1997): 729-742.

Allison, Ralph I., and Kenneth P. Uhl. "Influence of Beer Brand Identification on Taste Perception." *Journal of Marketing Research* 1 (1964): 36-39.

Bargh, John A., Mark Chen, and Lara Burrows. "Automaticity of Social Behavior: Direct Effects of Trait Construct and Stereotype Activation on Action." *Journal of Personality and Social Psychology* 71 (1996): 230-244.

Barovick, Harriet. "What's So Funny? Laughter-Yoga Fans Hail the Benefits of Giggling for No Reason." In *Time,* September 13, 2010, http://content.time.com/time/magazine/article/0,9171,2015766,00.html.

Barry, Thomas E., and Daniel J. Howard. "A Review and Critique of Hierarchy of Effects in Advertising." *International Journal of Advertising* 9, 2 (1990): 121-135.

Barthes, Roland. *The Pleasure of the Text*. New York: Hill and Wang, 1975.

Bechara, Antoine, Hanna Damasio, Daniel Tranel, and Antonio R. Damasio. "Deciding Advantageously Before Knowing the Advantageous Strategy." *Science* 235, 28 (February, 1997): 1293-1295.

Bem, Daryl J. "Self-Perception: An Alternative Interpretation of Cognitive Dissonance Phenomena." *Psychological Review,* 74 (1967): 183-200.

Berlyne, D.E. "A Theory of Human Curiosity." *British Journal of Psychology* 45:3 (1954): 180-191.

Bernbach, Bill. *Bill Bernbach Said*, http://www.ddb.com/pdf/bernbach.pdf, n.d.

Bikhchandani, Sushil, David Hirshleifer, and Ivo Welch. "Learning from the Behavior of Others: Conformity, Fads, and Informational Cascades." *Journal of Economic Perspectives* 12, Number 3 (Summer, 1998): 151-170.

Bowen, Deborah J., Naomi Tomoyasu, Marin Anderson, Maureen Carney, and Alan Kristal. "Effects of Expectancies and Personalized Feedback on Fat Consumption, Taste, and Preference." *Journal of Applied Social Psychology* 22 (1992): 1061-1079.

Brehm, Jack W. "Post Decision Changes in Desirability of Alternatives." *Social Psychology* 52 (1956): 384-389.

Brock, Timothy C., and Melanie C. Green. *Persuasion: Psychological Insights and Perspectives*. Thousand Oaks: Sage Publications, 2005.

Brown, Donald E. *Human Universals*. New York: McGraw-Hill, Inc., 1991.

Carnegie, Dale. *How to Win Friends and Influence People.* New York: Simon and Schuster, 1936.

Carney, Dana R., Amy J.C. Cuddy, and Andy J. Yap. "Power Posing: Brief Nonverbal Displays Affect Neuroendocrine Levels and Risk Tolerance." *Psychological Science* 21 (10) (2010): 1363-1368.

Cialdini, Robert B., PhD. *Influence: The Psychology of Persuasion.* New York: Harper Collins Publishers, 1984.

Cooper, Joel, Robert Mirabile, and Steven J. Scher. "Actions and Attitudes: The Theory of Cognitive Dissonance." In *Persuasion: Psychological Insights and Perspectives,* by Timothy C. Brock and Melanie C. Green. 63-80. Thousand Oaks, CA: Sage Publications, 2005.

Corey, S.M. "Professed Attitudes and Actual Behavior." *Journal of Educational Psychology* 28(4) (1937): 271-280.

Crimmins, J., and C. Callahan. "Reducing Road Rage: The Role of Target Insight in Advertising for Social Change." *Journal of Advertising Research* 43(4) (2003): 381-389.

Damasio, Antonio. *The Feeling of What Happens: Body and Emotion in the Making of Consciousness.* New York: Harcourt Brace. 1999.

Deighton, J. "The Interaction of Advertising and Evidence." *Journal of Consumer Research* 11 (December, 1984): 763-770.

Dijksterhuis, Ap, and John A. Bargh. "The Perception-Behavior Expressway: Automatic Effects of Social Perception on Social Behavior." *Advances in Experimental Social Psychology* 33 (2001): 1-40.

Eagleman, David. *Incognito: the Secret Lives of the Brain.* New York: Pantheon Books, a division of Random House, Inc., 2011.

Ehrenberg, Andrew, Gerald J. Goodhardt, and T. Patrick Barwise. "Double Jeopardy Revisited." *Journal of Marketing* 54 (July, 1990): 82-91.

Elbel, Brian, Rogan Kersh, Victoria L. Brescoll, and L. Beth Dixon. "Calorie Labeling And Food Choices: A First Look At The Effects On Low-Income People In New York City." *Health Affairs* 28(6) (2009): 1110-1121.

Festinger, Leon, and James M. Carlsmith. "Cognitive Consequences of Forced Compliance." *Journal of Abnormal and Social Psychology* 58(2) (1959): 203-210.

Fischhoff, Baruch, and Ruth Beyth (1975). "'I Knew it Would Happen': Remembered Probabilities of Once—Future Things." *Organizational Behavior and Human Performance* 13 (1975): 1-16.

Flaherty, Stacy, and Mimi Minnick. *Marlboro Oral History and Documentation Project, ca. 1926-1986.* http://americanhistory.si.edu/archives/d7198.htm, Smithsonian Institution, 2000.

Freedman, Jonathan L., and Scott C. Fraser. "Compliance Without Pressure: The Foot-In-The-Door Technique." *Journal of Personality and Social Psychology* 4, No. 2 (1966): 195-202.

Gazzaniga, Michael S. "Right Hemisphere Language Following Brain Bisection: A 20 Year Perspective." *American Psychologist* 38, No. 5 (May, 1983): 525-537.

Gentile, Elisabetta, and Scott A. Imberman. "Dressed for Success? The Effect of School Uniforms on Student Achievement and Behavior." *Journal of Urban Economics* 71(1) (2012): 1-17.

Gilovich, Thomas, Kenneth Savitsky, and Victoria Husted Medvec. "The Spotlight Effect in Social Judgment: An Egocentric Bias in Estimates of the Salience of One's Own Actions and Appearance." *Journal of Personality and Social Psychology* 78, No. 2, (2000): 211-221.

Goethe, Johann Wolfgang Von (1749-1832). German poet, novelist and dramatist, n.d.

Gombrich, E.H. *Art and Illusion*. Princeton, N.J.: Princeton University Press, 1960.

Grandy, Richard E., and Richard Warner. "Paul Grice." In *Stanford Encyclopedia of Philosophy*, edited by Edward N. Zalta. Stanford CA: The Metaphysics Research Lab, Center for the Study of Language and Information, Stanford University, 2009.

Gromet, Dena M., Howard Kunreuther, and Richard P. Larrick. "Political Ideology Affects Energy-Efficiency Attitudes and Choices." *Proceedings of the National Academy of Sciences USA* 110 (2013): 9314–9319.

Haidt, Jonathan. "The Emotional Dog and Its Rational Tail: A Social Intuitionist Approach to Moral Judgment." *Psychological Review* 108 (2001): 814-838.

Hair, Joseph, Mary Wolfinbarger, David Ortinau, and Robert Bush. *Essentials of Marketing Research*. Toronto, ON: McGraw-Hill, 2008.

Heath, Dr. Robert, and Paul Feldwick. "50 Years Using the Wrong Model of Advertising." *International Journal of Market Research* 50, Issue 1 (2008): 29-59.

Heider, Fritz. *The Psychology of Interpersonal Relations*. New York: Wiley, 1958.

Helman, Christopher. "David Crane's Green Vision For Carbon-Belching NRG Energy." *Forbes*, July 21, 2014, 1-2.

Hoch, Stephen J., and Young-Won Ha. "Consumer Learning: Advertising and the Ambiguity of Product Experience." *Journal of Consumer Research* 13, No. 2 (1986): 221-233.

Hoyer, Wayne D., and Steven P. Brown. "Effects of Brand Awareness on Choice for a Common, Repeat-Purchase Product." *Journal of Consumer Research* 17, No. 2 (Sep., 1990): 141-148.

James, William. *William James: Writings 1878-1899.* Cambridge, MA: Harvard University Press, 1984.

Kahneman, Daniel, and Amos Tversky. "Judgment under Uncertainty: Heuristics and Biases." *Science* 185 (September, 1974): 1124-1131.

Kahneman, Daniel. *Thinking Fast and Think Slow.* New York: Farrar, Straus and Giroux, 2011.

Klayman, Joshua, and Young-Won Ha. "Confirmation, Disconfirmation, and Information in Hypothesis Testing." *Psychological Review* XCIV (1987): 221-228.

Lee, Leonard, Shane Frederick, and Dan Ariely. "Try It, You'll Like It: The Influence of Expectation, Consumption, and Revelation on Preferences for Beer." *Association for Psychological Science* 17, No. 12 (2006): 1054-1058.

Leippe, Michael R., and Donna Eisenstadt. "Generalization of Dissonance Reduction: Decreasing Prejudice through Induced Compliance." *Journal of Personality and Social Psychology* 67 (1994): 395-413.

Lewicki, P., T. Hill, and E. Bizot. "Acquisition of Procedural Knowledge about a Pattern of Stimuli that Cannot Be Articulated." *Cognitive Psychology* 20 (1988): 24-37.

Li, Wen, Richard E. Zinbarg, Stephan G. Boehm, and Ken A. Paller. "Neural and Behavioral Evidence for Affective Priming from Unconsciously Perceived Emotional Facial Expressions and the Influence of Trait Anxiety." *Journal of Cognitive Neuroscience* 20:1 (2008): 95-107.

Libet, Benjamin. "Unconscious Cerebral Initiative and the Role of Conscious Will in Voluntary Action." *Behavioral and Brain Sciences* 8 (1985): 529-566.

Loewenstein, George. "Out of Control: Visceral Influences on Behavior." *Organizational Behavior and Human Decision Processes* 65, No. 3 (March, 1996): 272-292.

Lynch Jr., John G., and Gal Zauberman. "When Do You Want It? Time, Decisions, and Public Policy." *Journal of Public Policy and Marketing* 25 (1) (Spring, 2006): 67-78.

Makens, James C. "Effect of Brand Preference upon Consumers' Perceived Taste of Turkey Meat." *Journal of Applied Psychology* 49 (1965): 261-263.

Maslow, A.H. "A Theory of Human Motivation." *Psychological Review* 50 (1943): 370-396.

McClure, Samuel M., Jian Li, Damon Tomlin, Kim S. Cypert, Latane M. Montague, and P. Read Montague. "Neural Correlates of Behavior Preference for Culturally Familiar Drinks." *Neuron* 44 (Oct. 14, 2004): 379-387.

McQuarrie, Edward F., and David Glen Mick. "Figures of Rhetoric in Advertising Language." *The Journal of Consumer Research* 22, No. 4 (1996): 424-438.

Mehrabian, Albert, and Morton Wiener. "Decoding of Inconsistent Communications." *Journal of Personality and Social Psychology* 6 (1), (1967): 109-114.

Mehrabian, Albert, and Susan R. Ferris. "Inference of Attitudes from Nonverbal Communication in Two Channels." *Journal of Consulting Psychology*, June 31(3), (1967): 248-252.

Miller, Jonathan. "Going Unconscious." *New York Review of Books.* April 20, 1995.

Neal, David T., Wendy Wood, and Jeffrey M. Quinn. "Habits—A Repeat Performance." *Current Directions in Psychological Science* 15, No. 4 (2006): 198-202.

Nevid, Jeffrey S. "Effects of Brand Labeling on Ratings of Product Quality." *Perceptual and Motor Skills* 53 (1981): 407-410.

Nisbett, Richard E., and Timothy DeCamp Wilson. "Telling More Than We Can Know: Verbal Reports on Mental Processes." *Psychological Review* 84 (1977): 231-259.

Norretranders, Tor. *The User Illusion*. New York: Viking, 1991.

O'Donoghue, Ted, and Matthew Rabin. "Doing It Now or Later." *The American Economic Review* 89, No. 1 (March, 1999): 103-124.

Olson, Jerry C., and Philip A. Dover. "Cognitive Effects of Deceptive Advertising." *Journal of Marketing Research* 15 (1978): 29-38.

Plous, Scott. *The Psychology of Judgment and Decision Making*. New York: McGraw-Hill, Inc., 1993.

Pomiankowski, A. "How to Find the Top Male." *Nature* 347 (1990): 616-617.

Ridley, Matt. *The Red Queen: Sex and the Evolution of Human Nature*. Great Britain: Penguin Books Ltd., 1993.

Rogers, Will. *Saturday Evening Post*, November 6, 1926.

Rogers, Richard, and Oscar Hammerstein. Lyrics to "Some Enchanted Evening." *South Pacific*. http://www.lyricsmode. com/lyrics/r/rodgers_and_hammerstein/some_enchant- ed_evening.html.

Robinson, Thomas N., Dina L.G. Borzekowski, Donna M. Matheson, and Helena C.

Kraemer. "Effects of Fast Food Branding on Young Children's Taste Preferences." *Archives of Pediatric Adolescent Medicine*. 161(8) (2007): 792-797.

Salgonic, Matthew J., Peter Sheridan Dodds, and Duncan J. Watts. "Experimental Study of Inequality and Unpredictability in an Artificial Cultural Market." *Science* 311 (2006): 854-856.

Sherman, Steven J. "On the Self-Erasing Nature of Errors of Prediction." *Journal of Personality and Social Psychology* 39 (1980): 211-221.

Slovic, Paul, Melissa L. Finucane, Ellen Peters, and Donald G. MacGregor. "The Affect Heuristic." In *Heuristics and Biases:*

The Psychology of Intuitive Judgment. Edited by Thomas Gilovitch and Daniel Kahneman. 397-420. New York: Cambridge University Press, 2002.

Soon, Chun Siong, Marcel Brass, Hans-Jochen Heinze, and John-Dylan Haynes. "Unconscious Determinants of Free Decisions in the Human Brain." *Nature Neuroscience* 11(5) (April 13, 2008): 543-545.

Sperber, Dan, and Deirdre Wilson. *Relevance: Communication and Cognition, 2nd ed.* Oxford: Blackwell Publishers Ltd, 1995.

Thaler, Richard H., and Cass R. Sunstein. "Easy Does It." *The New Republic*, April 8, 2008. https://newrepublic.com/article/63355/easy-does-it.

Thaler, Richard H., and Cass R. Sunstein. *Nudge: Improving Decisions About Health, Wealth, and Happiness.* New Haven: Yale University Press, 2008.

"Throwing Out the Free Market Playbook: An Interview with Naomi Klein," *Solutions* 3, 1 (February, 2012), http://www.thesolutionsjournal.com/node/1053.

Tversky, Amos, and Daniel Kahneman. "Rational Choice and the Framing of Decisions." *The Journal of Business* 59, No. 4, Part 2 *The Behavioral Foundations of Economic Theory,* (1986): S251-S278.

Twain, Mark. *The Adventures of Tom Sawyer.* Page By Page Books, 1876. http://www.pagebypagebooks.com/Mark_Twain/Tom_Sawyer/.

Vonnegut, Kurt. *Mother Night.* New York: Delacorte Press/ Seymour Lawrence, 1961.

Wansink, Brian, Sea Bum Park, Steven Sonka, and Michelle Morganosky. "How Soy Labeling Influences Preference and Taste." *International Food and Agribusiness Management Review* 3 (2000): 85-94.

Wansink, Brian, Sea Bum Park, Steven Sonka, and Michelle Morganosky. "Slim by Design: Kitchen Counter Correlates of Obesity." *Health Education and Behavior.* (October 19, 2015): 85-94.

Wardle, Jane, and Wendy Solomons. "Naughty but Nice: A Laboratory Study of Health Information and Food Preferences in a Community Sample." *Health Psychology* 13 (1994): 180-183.

Wegner, Daniel M., and Thalia Wheatley. "Apparent Mental Causation: Sources of the Experience of Will." *American Psychologist* 54 (1999): 480-492.

Wicker, Allan W. "Attitudes versus Actions: The Relationship of Verbal and Overt Behavioral Responses to Attitude Objects." *Journal of Social Issues* XXV, Number 4, (1969): 41-78.

Wilson, Timothy D. *Strangers to Ourselves.* Cambridge, Massachusetts: The Belknap Press of Harvard University Press, 2002.

Wood, Orlando. "How Emotional Tugs Trump Rational Pushes: The Time Has Come to Abandon a 100-Year Old Advertising Model." *Journal of Advertising Research.* (March, 2012): 31-39.

Zajonc, Robert B. "Attitudinal Effects of Mere Exposure." *Journal of Personality and Social Psychology* 9 (2 Pt. 2) (1968): 1-27.

Zimbardo, Philip G., Matisyohu Weisenberg, Ira Firestone, and Burton Levy. "Communicator Effectiveness in Producing Public Conformity and Private Attitude Change." *Journal of Personality* 33 (1965): 233-255.

INDEX